Spiritual Abundance
Unlocking the Power of the Holy Spirit Gifts and
Nurturing His Fruit!

Harrison Sharma Mungal, PhD., Psy.D.

Spiritual Abundance

Copyright © 2024 Harrison S. Mungal

All rights reserved. Neither this publication nor any part of this publication may be reproduced or transmitted in any form or by any means, electronic or mechanical, including photocopying, recording or any information storage and retrieval system, without permission in writing from the author.

Unless otherwise identified, Scripture quotations are from New King James Version of the Bible.

Contact author via email:
info@harrisonmungal.com
info@agetoage.ca
www.agetoage.ca
www.harrisonmungal.com
www.harrisonmungalbooks.com
Facebook: Harrison Mungal
Twitter: AgeToAgeInc1
LinkedIn: Harrison Mungal, Ph.D., PsyD
YouTube: Harrison Mungal
Phone: 905-533-1334

ABOUT the AUTHOR

Harrison Sharma Mungal, BTh, MCC, MSW, PhD, PsyD

Dr. Mungal is a devoted therapist with a background in mental health and clinical psychology, driven by a genuine passion for life and the well-being of those under his care. With an impressive literary portfolio comprising over 40 books and a seasoned public speaking career that has reached audiences in over 42 nations, he brings a wealth of knowledge and skills to his practice.

Alongside his professional accomplishments, Dr. Mungal places a high value on family, with a successful marriage of over 34 years, seven children, and multiple grandchildren. In addition to his clinical practice, Dr. Mungal and his wife have played pivotal roles in church planting, pastoral ministry, and missionary work, even during the challenging times of the Cold War in Croatia from 1994-1997. They have nurtured congregations, established churches, and served as missionaries, demonstrating a deep commitment to spreading the gospel. Their dedication extended to running a Bible college, Metro Bible College, for over a decade before transitioning into mental health and addictions counselling.

Dr. Mungal is widely respected for his unique ability to blend biblical principles with scientific insights, adding a distinctive "psychology twist" to his therapeutic approach. He explained God made us Body, Soul (mind, will and emotions) and Spirit. As much as people need support physically and spiritually, "the soul is where people are wounded and is in need of healing." His expertise has been sought after by various media outlets, including appearances on television programs including 700 Clubs Canada and 100 Huntly St. He has also been invited to speak at prestigious institutions such as the Attorney General of Canada, police departments, hospitals, community agencies, and churches. His contributions have earned him accolades and recognition from local authorities, police departments, mayors, community leaders, and countless families.

With over 21 years of experience in mental health, psychiatry, and psychology, coupled with over four decades dedicated to teaching and preaching the gospel, Dr. Mungal possesses a wealth of expertise in both fields. His educational background is equally impressive, with a Christian Leadership Certificate, a Ministerial Diploma from two years of Bible College, a bachelor's degree in Theology, two master's degrees (in Counselling and Social Work), and two doctorate degrees (in Social Work and Clinical Psychology).

In summary, Dr. Mungal's journey is a testament to his unwavering commitment to serving others, integrating his faith with his professional expertise to make a positive impact in the lives of countless individuals, couples, and families. His multifaceted career reflects a deep sense of purpose and a profound dedication to promoting holistic healing and spiritual growth.

Table of Contents

INTRODUCTION 9
GIFTS OF THE SPIRIT 11
THE GIFT OF TONGUES 15
THE GIFT OF INTERPRETATION OF TONGUES 35
THE GIFT OF PROPHECY 41
THE GIFT OF KNOWLEDGE 49
THE GIFT OF WISDOM 57
THE GIFT OF DISCERNING OF SPIRITS 65
THE GIFT OF FAITH 71
THE GIFT OF WORKING MIRACLES 75
THE GIFTS OF HEALING 79
FRUIT OF THE SPIRIT 85
LOVE 87
JOY 95

PEACE	101
LONGSUFFERING	107
MEEKNESS or KINDNESS	113
GOODNESS	117
FAITHFULNESS	121
GENTLENESS	125
TEMPERANCE OR SELF-CONTROL	127
CONCLUSION	133

INTRODUCTION

Spiritual Abundance - Unlocking the Power of the Holy Spirit Gifts and Nurturing His Fruit!" explores the transformative power of the Holy Spirit in our lives. These gifts, bestowed upon us by the Spirit, are not merely for our own benefit but are meant to enrich the lives of those around us.

The Apostle Paul beautifully articulates the diversity of these gifts in Corinthians, reminding us that each of us has been endowed with unique manifestations of the Spirit. From the word of wisdom to the gift of healing, from the discerning of spirits to speaking in tongues, these gifts are divine expressions of the Spirit's presence and power in our lives.

But alongside these remarkable gifts, we also encounter the fruit of the Spirit—a bouquet of virtues that blossom within us as we walk in step with the Holy Spirit. Love, joy, peace, patience, kindness, goodness, faithfulness, gentleness, and self-control—these are the fruits that adorn the branches of our spiritual journey, nourished by the life-giving sap of the Holy Spirit.

Just as a tree bears fruit according to its nature, so too do we, as believers, bear the fruit of the Spirit as we abide in Him. Each fruit is a testament to the transformative work of the Holy Spirit in our hearts, shaping us into vessels of love, vessels of joy, vessels of peace, and vessels of all the other virtues that reflect the character of Christ.

In this exploration of spiritual abundance, we will uncover the profound significance of both the gifts and fruits of the Spirit. We'll learn how to cultivate these gifts, allowing them to flourish and impact the world around us. We'll also discover the importance of nurturing the fruit of the Spirit, tending to the garden of our hearts so that it may yield a bountiful harvest of spiritual virtues.

So, come along on this journey of discovery and transformation as we unlock the power of the Holy Spirit gifts and nurture His fruit. Together, let's embrace the abundance that awaits us and allow the Spirit to work mightily in our lives for the glory of God and the flourishing of His kingdom.

GIFTS OF THE SPIRIT

Welcome to an exploration of "The Gifts of the Holy Spirit"! I'm excited to journey with you as we delve into the supernatural endowments bestowed upon believers for service in the Body of Christ.

The gifts of the Spirit are divine manifestations given according to the character of the ministry to be fulfilled. Their ultimate purpose is to edify and build up the Church, reflecting the multifaceted nature of God's power and grace. As believers, our first pursuit should always be Jesus, the source of the Holy Spirit and the bestower of these gifts.

In 1 Corinthians 12:31, we're encouraged to earnestly desire the best gifts, recognizing the potential for greater works to be done through us by the power of the Holy Spirit. Jesus Himself promised that believers would do even greater works

GIFTS OF THE SPIRIT

than He did during His earthly ministry, thanks to the indwelling presence of the Spirit.

The gifts of the Spirit encompass various aspects, including administrations (different kinds of service) and operations (different workings). Each gift is uniquely distributed by the Holy Spirit, empowering individuals to fulfill their calling and contribute to the work of God in the world.

It's important to distinguish between the gifts of the Spirit and natural talents or abilities. While both are gifts from God, the supernatural manifestations of the Holy Spirit operate beyond the realm of human capability. These gifts are activated by the Spirit's will and are evidence of His presence and power in the lives of believers.

Throughout history, believers baptized in the Holy Spirit have demonstrated the gifts through supernatural manifestations, such as speaking in tongues and prophesying. These manifestations serve as confirmation of God's power at work in their ministries, providing spiritual weaponry to address the world's challenges.

While the gifts of the Spirit are powerful, they are also accompanied by the fruits of the Spirit. Love, joy, peace, longsuffering, gentleness, and goodness are among the virtues that complement and enhance the exercise of spiritual gifts. Together, they equip believers for impactful service in the kingdom of God.

As we explore the nine gifts of the Spirit—Utterance Gifts (*Diversity of tongues, Interpretation of tongues, Gifts of Prophecy*), Revelation Gifts (*Word of Knowledge, Word of Wisdom, Discerning of Spirits*), and Power Gifts (*Gifts of Healing, Working of Miracles, Gift of Faith*)—may we approach them with reverence and expectation, recognizing their potential for transformation and empowerment in our lives and in the world around us.

Imagine the church as a bustling construction site, with each spiritual gift serving as a vital tool in erecting a strong, vibrant community of faith. Just as a skilled worker knows how to use their tools safely and efficiently, so too must I learn to wield my spiritual gifts in a manner that benefits the entire body of believers.

Paul's instructions provide a roadmap for navigating the use of spiritual gifts within the church. It's akin to receiving hands-on training from a seasoned craftsman who imparts invaluable wisdom on wielding each tool with precision and care. I'm eager to grasp these teachings, knowing they will equip me to contribute meaningfully to the edification of the church.

Through Paul's guidance, I learn that exercising spiritual gifts isn't about showcasing personal prowess or seeking attention. Instead, it's about selflessly serving others and glorifying God. Just as a skilled artisan focuses on the greater goal of constructing a sturdy building, I'm called to direct my efforts toward the collective growth and unity of the church.

GIFTS OF THE SPIRIT

As I immerse myself in Paul's instructions, I'm reminded of the importance of humility and cooperation within the body of believers. Each member plays a unique role, and when we work together harmoniously, our collective efforts yield a beautiful masterpiece that reflects God's glory.

Ultimately, Paul's teachings on handling spiritual gifts serve as a reminder that our individual contributions, when guided by love and humility, contribute to the greater work of God's kingdom. With this understanding, I approach the use of my spiritual gifts with reverence, seeking to uplift and strengthen the church community with every action. These gifts are not just for show; they're meant to empower us in the body of Christ.

After Paul emphasized that spiritual gifts are meant to build up the church, much like scaffolding supports a building during construction, I feel compelled to understand how to handle these gifts responsibly and effectively within the church community.

THE GIFT OF **TONGUES**

You know, the gift of tongues is something I find truly remarkable. It's like this amazing ability that God gives us to speak in different languages, almost as if He's unlocking this hidden talent within us. When I speak in tongues, it feels like a direct connection to heaven, like I'm conversing with God in this special language that's just between us. It's pure, it's powerful, and it's one of the most profound experiences of the Spirit working in me. On the day of Pentecost, the gift of tongues and its interpretation were bestowed upon believers.

Firstly, tongues are a God-given gift, plain and simple. It's like He's handing me this incredible ability to communicate in languages I've never learned, and it's nothing short of miraculous. It's like He's saying, "Here's a way for you to speak directly to Me, no matter where you are or what language you speak."

THE GIFT OF TONGUES

Secondly, tongues are like a vocal miracle straight from God. When I speak in tongues, it's like I can feel His presence surrounding me, guiding my words and filling me with His Spirit. It's a reminder of His power and His constant presence in my life.

Thirdly, tongues are this heavenly prayer language that transcends earthly limitations. It's like I'm tapping into this deeper level of communication with God, where words aren't necessary, and my heart speaks directly to His. It's a language of love, of worship, and of intimate connection with my Creator.

And you know what's incredible? Tongues are this pure, unfiltered expression of my spirit connecting with the Holy Spirit. It's like stripping away all the noise and distractions of the world and communing with God on the most fundamental level. It's simple, it's sincere, and it's profoundly beautiful.

Finally, tongues are one of the most powerful manifestations of the Spirit within me. When I speak in tongues, it's like I can feel His presence moving in and through me, filling me with His strength and His wisdom. It's a reminder that I'm never alone, that He's always with me, guiding me and empowering me to live out His purpose for my life.

You know, when I think about the significance of tongues as a sign of the New Covenant, I can't help but reflect on Pentecost. It's this special time, different from other feasts, because it uses leavened bread instead of unleavened. And it was during this unique celebration that the Holy Spirit was poured out on everyday people like me, flawed and imperfect as we are.

Pentecost wasn't just another holiday; it was a momentous occasion, a turning point in history. It was when God chose to reveal His Spirit in a powerful way, not just to a select few, but to everyone who believed. And I'm one of those believers, someone who has experienced the transformative power of the Holy Spirit in my own life.

You see, Pentecost wasn't just about tongues; it was about the birth of the Church, about God ushering in a new era of His kingdom on earth. And tongues played a crucial role in this, serving as a sign of God's presence and His desire to unite people from every nation, tribe, and tongue.

As I reflect on Pentecost and the significance of tongues, I'm reminded that God's plan is so much bigger than I can imagine. It's about breaking down barriers, bridging divides, and bringing people together in unity and love. And tongues are just one way that God is making this vision a reality in my life and in the world around me.

When I think about the gift of tongues and its significance as a sign of the end of Babel, it's like seeing a beautiful tapestry woven together from threads of different colours and textures.

THE GIFT OF TONGUES

This gift, which first appeared in the New Covenant, is like a beacon of hope, signaling God's reversal of the language confusion that originated at Babel.

I can't help but be amazed at how God works in mysterious ways, using something as simple as language to demonstrate His power and wisdom. In the book of Acts, we see how the gift of tongues was bestowed upon the early believers, empowering them to communicate the message of God's love and redemption to people from every nation and tongue.

It's incredible to think about how, through the Church, God is bringing people together in unity and harmony, despite our differences in language and culture. The gift of tongues serves as a reminder that, in Christ, we are all part of one body, united by our faith and love for Him.

As I reflect on the gift of tongues and its significance in the grand narrative of God's redemption, I'm reminded of His faithfulness and sovereignty. Just as He reversed the language confusion at Babel, He continues to work in our lives today, bringing beauty and unity out of diversity and discord.

When I reflect on the gift of tongues, I see it as a tangible sign of God's control over my life as a believer. It's like a gentle nudge from the Holy Spirit, guiding my words and actions in alignment with God's purpose for me. Acts 2:26 speaks to me deeply, reminding me that when the Holy Spirit takes control, my heart overflows with joy, and my speech reflects His presence within me.

SPIRITUAL ABUNDANCE

The gift of tongues also highlights the significance of taming the tongue, as James 3:8-10 emphasizes. It's a powerful reminder of the transformative work the Holy Spirit does within me, enabling me to control my speech and use it to glorify God. This control isn't something I achieve on my own; it's a gift from God, made possible by His Spirit dwelling within me.

When I speak in tongues, I'm reminded of God's sovereignty over every aspect of my life. It's a beautiful expression of His presence within me, guiding me and empowering me to live in obedience to His will. Just as a bridle controls a horse or a rudder steers a ship, the gift of tongues serves as a tangible reminder of God's control over my entire being.

In those moments of speaking in tongues, I feel a deep sense of connection to God, knowing that He is at work within me, shaping me into the person He created me to be. It's a humbling experience, recognizing that I am surrendered to His leading and empowered by His Spirit.

When I reflect on the account of the Gentiles receiving the Holy Spirit at Cornelius' house in Acts 10, it fills me with awe and wonder at the inclusivity of God's love. In that moment, cultural and linguistic barriers were shattered as the Holy Spirit descended upon these Gentiles, just as He had upon the Jews at Pentecost.

THE GIFT OF TONGUES

The scene at Cornelius' house serves as a powerful reminder of God's boundless grace and His desire for all people to experience His Spirit. As I picture Cornelius and his household receiving the Holy Spirit and speaking in tongues, I'm reminded that God's love knows no bounds. He reaches out to everyone, regardless of their background or heritage, inviting them into a personal relationship with Him.

Witnessing the Gentiles speaking in tongues affirmed for the Jewish believers present that God's Spirit was truly at work in these Gentile hearts. It was a moment of divine confirmation, demonstrating that the same Spirit who had empowered them at Pentecost was now empowering these Gentile believers as well.

The outpouring of the Holy Spirit at Cornelius' house challenges me to embrace God's inclusive love and to recognize that His Spirit is at work in unexpected places and among unexpected people. It's a reminder to me that God's kingdom knows no boundaries and that His Spirit is moving in powerful ways to draw all people to Himself.

Thinking about the disciples at Ephesus in Acts 19:1-7 always leaves me in awe of the power and presence of the Holy Spirit. When Paul laid his hands on these followers of John the Baptist, something extraordinary happened. They began to speak in tongues and prophesy, revealing the Spirit's transformative work in their lives.

SPIRITUAL ABUNDANCE

As I ponder this scene, I'm struck by the significance of the disciples' response to the Holy Spirit. Speaking in tongues and prophesying were not just random occurrences; they were profound expressions of God's presence and power. It's as if the Spirit ignited a fire within them, igniting their hearts with a fervent desire to proclaim God's truth to the world.

The fact that speaking in tongues and prophesying are mentioned separately in the text highlights the multifaceted nature of the Holy Spirit's work. Each gift serves a unique purpose in building up the body of Christ and spreading the gospel message. It's a reminder to me that God equips each of us with specific gifts to fulfill His purposes in the world.

The disciples at Ephesus teach me that encountering the Holy Spirit is not just a one-time event; it's an ongoing journey of transformation and empowerment. Just as the disciples experienced the Spirit's power in their lives, I too can experience His presence in a profound and life-changing way.

Reflecting on the role of tongues in the everyday life of the church, I'm reminded of the guidance found in 1 Corinthians chapters 12 to 14. Unlike the unique occurrences of tongues we've seen previously, these passages offer insight into how tongues function within the regular rhythm of church life.

In these chapters, Paul provides practical instructions and insights into the use of tongues within the community of believers. It's like he's offering a roadmap for incorporating

THE GIFT OF TONGUES

this spiritual gift into our gatherings in a way that edifies and uplifts the body of Christ.

As I delve into Paul's teachings, I find myself struggling with questions about how tongues should be exercised within the context of our worship and fellowship. How do we balance the spontaneity of the Spirit with the need for order and understanding? How can we ensure that tongues are used to build up the church rather than cause confusion?

Paul's words challenge me to approach the gift of tongues with humility, seeking the guidance of the Holy Spirit as we navigate its place in our communal worship. It's a reminder that spiritual gifts are meant to be exercised in love and with the purpose of edifying the body of Christ.

As I seek to apply Paul's teachings to my own church experience, I'm inspired to create an atmosphere where the gifts of the Spirit can flow freely, yet with discernment and order. It's a journey of discovery and growth as we seek to honor God and build up one another in faith.

As I explore 1 Corinthians 12, I encounter a fascinating discussion about the various gifts of the Spirit, including the gift of tongues and the interpretation of tongues. These verses shed light on the distinction between speaking in tongues and interpreting them, highlighting that these abilities are separate and distinct from our everyday language skills.

Unlike our natural ability to speak and understand languages, the gifts of tongues and interpretation operate on a supernatural level, bestowed by the Holy Spirit for the benefit of the entire church community. It's like God equips His people with these gifts as tools to build up and strengthen the body of believers.

As I ponder this distinction, I'm struck by the communal nature of these gifts. They're not given for individual glory or personal gain but are intended to serve the greater good of the church as a whole. It's as if God is orchestrating a beautiful symphony within His church, with each gift playing its unique part in creating harmony and unity.

Reflecting on these verses, I'm reminded of the importance of embracing the diversity of gifts within the body of Christ. Just as each instrument in an orchestra contributes to the overall melody, so too do the gifts of tongues and interpretation add depth and richness to our spiritual journey together.

In essence, these gifts remind me that we are all interconnected members of the same body, each contributing our unique talents and abilities for the common good. And as we honor and celebrate the diverse gifts of the Spirit, we create space for God's power and presence to move among us in transformative ways.

In 1 Corinthians 13, I find myself struggling with a common misconception: that love trumps all and renders spiritual gifts inconsequential. However, upon closer examination, I realize that Paul's message is much deeper than that. He's emphasizing the critical role of attitudes in

THE GIFT OF TONGUES

determining the effectiveness of these gifts within the church community.

Paul isn't dismissing the importance of spiritual gifts; rather, he's highlighting the need for the right mindset to accompany their use. It's as if he's reminding us that the value of these gifts lies not just in their manifestation but in the spirit with which they're exercised.

As I reflect on this, I'm struck by the notion that gifts, no matter how extraordinary, are ultimately temporary. They're like tools designed for a specific purpose—to build up and strengthen the church. And just as a carpenter uses tools with skill and care, so too must we approach the exercise of spiritual gifts with the right attitude.

In essence, Paul's message serves as a gentle reminder that love is the foundation upon which all spiritual gifts must be exercised. Without love as our guiding principle, these gifts lose their potency and fail to fulfill their intended purpose of edifying the body of Christ.

So, as I navigate my own journey of faith and service within the church, I'm challenged to cultivate a heart of love—a heart that values others above myself, seeks the best for my brothers and sisters, and honours God in all that I do. And as I do so, I trust that the gifts of the Spirit will flow through me in ways that bring glory to His name and blessing to His people.

In 1 Corinthians 13:1, I'm struck by the intriguing mention of tongues of angels. This notion challenges the traditional understanding of tongues as earthly languages and opens up a realm of possibility—that the tongues spoken could transcend human comprehension and be heavenly in nature.

The idea of tongues of angels suggests a deeper, more mystical aspect to the gift of speaking in tongues. It invites me to ponder the mysteries of the spiritual realm and the potential for communication beyond the confines of human language.

As I reflect on this concept, I find myself drawn into a sense of wonder and awe. Could it be that when I speak in tongues, I'm tapping into a language that transcends the earthly realm and connects me directly to the divine?

The thought of communicating in the language of angels fills me with a sense of reverence and humility. It reminds me that the Holy Spirit's work in my life is not limited by human understanding but reaches into the very depths of the heavenly realm.

In embracing the possibility of tongues as those of angels, I'm reminded of the boundless nature of God's kingdom and the unfathomable ways in which He chooses to reveal Himself to His people. It's a reminder to approach the gift of tongues with reverence and openness, knowing that it's a sacred and mysterious aspect of my spiritual journey.

In 1 Corinthians 13:1, I find Paul's emphasis on the importance of using the gift of tongues with love resonating deeply within me. It's a reminder that the way I use this gift matters just as much as the gift itself. Without love, my words,

THE GIFT OF TONGUES

even if they're spoken in tongues, can become nothing more than a distracting noise.

Paul's analogy of a clashing noise paints a vivid picture of what happens when tongues are not infused with love. It's like trying to listen to a cacophony of sounds that only serve to confuse and disrupt rather than uplift and edify. It makes me pause and reflect on the significance of love in every aspect of my spiritual expression, including the use of spiritual gifts.

As I ponder further, I realize that the effectiveness of my prayers, including speaking in tongues, is directly tied to the quality of my love for God. It's not just about the words I speak or the sounds I make; it's about the depth of my connection with God and the sincerity of my heart.

This principle extends beyond tongues to all the gifts of the Spirit. Whether it's prophecy, healing, or any other gift, if it's not motivated by love, it loses its power and purpose. Paul's words serve as a gentle reminder to me to cultivate a heart filled with love, for it is love that breathes life and meaning into everything I do in service to God and others.

Looking at 1 Corinthians 13:8, I'm reminded that, like other spiritual gifts, tongues will eventually cease. There are those who argue that this cessation occurred with the passing of the last of the twelve apostles. They believe that the "perfect" mentioned in 1 Corinthians 13:10 refers to the "completed canon of scripture," signifying the culmination of our understanding.

SPIRITUAL ABUNDANCE

However, as I delve into Scripture, I find no explicit mention of such a definitive completion of the canon. In fact, Revelation 22:18-19 warns against adding or taking away from the words of the book, suggesting that the concept of a closed canon may not be so clear-cut.

Upon further reflection, I see how 1 Corinthians 13:12 sheds light on the interpretation of verses 9 and 10. It speaks of our current state of partial understanding, implying that the "perfect" refers to the ultimate fulfillment of God's kingdom, rather than the completion of the Bible.

Moreover, viewing tongues solely in terms of knowledge misses the essence of their purpose. Tongues are a form of prayer, a direct line of communication between me and God (1 Corinthians 14:2). They transcend intellectual comprehension, offering a channel for spiritual expression and communion with the divine.

In delving into the topic of tongues within the church, I come across 1 Corinthians 14:2, which sheds light on the nature of these utterances. It's fascinating to learn that when someone speaks in tongues, they are actually communicating directly with God, expressing mysteries that transcend human understanding. This notion is further emphasized in verse 16, where it becomes clear that tongues are often used for giving thanks to God.

As I ponder these verses, I realize that the tongues spoken in the church setting differ from those witnessed at Pentecost.

THE GIFT OF TONGUES

During Pentecost, tongues were employed to glorify God in a way that could be comprehended by those present—they were actual languages understood by people from different regions. In contrast, the tongues spoken in the church seem to be veiled in mystery, with no one present able to grasp their meaning. Instead, they serve as a form of prayer and thanksgiving directed towards God.

This distinction between Pentecostal tongues and those heard in the church prompts me to reflect on the multifaceted nature of spiritual gifts. While both types of tongues originate from the Holy Spirit, they serve different purposes within the context of worship. It's a reminder that God's ways often transcend our understanding, and His Spirit works in diverse ways to achieve His purposes.

As I continue to explore the significance of tongues in the church, I'm struck by the profound mystery and reverence associated with this gift. Though the content of tongues may remain elusive to human comprehension, their role in facilitating intimate communication between the individual and God is undeniable. It's a testament to the depth of our relationship with the divine and the boundless expressions of worship that emerge from it.

In light of these insights, I approach the topic of tongues with a sense of awe and humility, recognizing that even when words fail to convey meaning to others, they hold profound significance in the realm of spiritual communion. Through tongues, I find a pathway to connect with God on a deeper

SPIRITUAL ABUNDANCE

level, expressing gratitude and reverence in a language that transcends the limitations of human speech.

As I explore Paul's teachings on tongues and prophecy, I find myself drawn to 1 Corinthians 14:1-5, where he shares his perspective on these spiritual gifts. While prophecy is esteemed for its ability to edify the entire church community, tongues, Paul suggests, serve a different purpose. Unlike prophecy, which benefits the collective body of believers, the primary function of tongues is to spiritually fortify the individual who speaks in them.

This revelation prompts me to reflect on the essence of tongues as a form of prayer. Unlike prophecy, which involves speaking forth divine messages for the benefit of others, tongues are a direct channel of communication between the believer and God. When I engage in tongues, I'm not only expressing my devotion to the divine but also receiving spiritual strength and empowerment in return.

Paul's distinction between tongues and prophecy underscores the personal nature of this gift. While prophecy serves to uplift and guide the entire congregation, tongues offer a unique opportunity for personal communion with the divine. In essence, tongues serve as a spiritual exercise that strengthens my inner being, equipping me for the challenges and opportunities of my faith journey.

As I contemplate the significance of tongues in my spiritual life, I recognize the transformative power they hold. Through

THE GIFT OF TONGUES

the act of speaking in tongues, I'm able to tap into a reservoir of spiritual strength and renewal, enabling me to navigate life's complexities with greater resilience and faith. It's a reminder that while prophecy may edify the community, tongues serve as a lifeline for my personal connection to God.

As I immerse myself in Paul's teachings on the gift of tongues, I'm struck by his emphasis on seeking the ability to interpret one's own utterances. In 1 Corinthians 14:13, he urges tongue-speakers, myself included, to pray fervently for the power to understand and interpret the tongues they speak. This command carries a sense of personal responsibility, as if Paul is urging me to actively engage in seeking this gift for myself.

Paul's words paint a vivid picture of the dynamic between the spirit and the mind during the act of speaking in tongues. While the spirit is engaged in fervent prayer, the mind remains idle and unfruitful (1 Corinthians 14:14). Yet, Paul doesn't see this state of mindlessness as desirable or beneficial for the tongue-speaker (1 Corinthians 14:15). Instead, he encourages me to seek self-interpretation, ensuring that both my spirit and my mind are edified during this spiritual practice.

The goal, it seems, is to align the spiritual and intellectual aspects of my being in a harmonious way. By seeking the ability to interpret my own tongues, I can avoid the pitfalls of a passive mind and instead experience a deepened connection with God. This proactive approach not only enriches my personal spiritual experience but also enables me to edify others by sharing the interpretation of my tongues with them (1 Corinthians 14:16-17).

In essence, Paul's guidance underscores the importance of engaging both my spirit and my mind in the practice of tongues. Rather than allowing my mind to remain idle, I'm encouraged to seek understanding and interpretation, thereby deepening my spiritual growth and enriching the communal experience of worship. It's a reminder that the gift of tongues is not passive but rather an active, transformative practice that engages every aspect of my being.

As I explore Paul's personal reflections on the gift of tongues, I find myself drawn to his candid admission about his own usage of this spiritual practice. In 1 Corinthians 14:18-19, Paul reveals that he speaks in tongues more frequently than anyone else in Corinth. It's a surprising revelation that offers a glimpse into Paul's deeply spiritual life and his intimate connection with the Holy Spirit.

Despite his proficiency in tongues, Paul expresses a clear preference for using language that is understood by others, especially within the context of the church. While he values the personal edification and spiritual communion that speaking in tongues brings, he recognizes the importance of clear communication and mutual understanding in the communal worship setting.

Paul's words resonate with me on a personal level, prompting me to reflect on my own experiences with the gift

THE GIFT OF TONGUES

of tongues. Like Paul, I may find solace and spiritual renewal in the practice of tongues during my private moments of prayer and devotion. Yet, when it comes to worshipping alongside my fellow believers, I understand the importance of using language that can be comprehended by all, fostering unity and edification within the community.

In Paul's example, I see a balance between personal spirituality and communal responsibility. While he cherishes the gift of tongues for its profound connection with the divine, he also recognizes the need for clarity and understanding in the shared worship experience. As I navigate my own spiritual journey, I strive to emulate Paul's wisdom, embracing the gift of tongues as a source of personal enrichment while remaining mindful of its impact on the larger community of believers.

Reflecting on the Corinthians' struggle with spiritual gifts, I realize the importance of mature thinking in the use of these gifts within the church community. In Paul's letter to the Corinthians, he addresses their lack of maturity in understanding and utilizing spiritual gifts effectively. Instead of using these gifts to build up the church, the Corinthians were inadvertently causing harm and division.

As I ponder on this, I can't help but empathize with the Corinthians' predicament. In their zeal and enthusiasm for spiritual experiences, they overlooked the need for discernment and wisdom in their expression of spiritual gifts. By all speaking in tongues simultaneously, they created confusion and chaos, alienating those who were unfamiliar with their practices.

Paul's admonition serves as a gentle reminder to me that spiritual gifts are meant to edify and unify the body of Christ, not to cause disorder or alienation. Just as the Corinthians needed to mature in their thinking about spiritual gifts, I too must approach these gifts with wisdom and maturity, considering their impact on the larger church community.

Ultimately, I understand that the goal of spiritual gifts is to attract unbelievers to Christ, not to drive them away. Therefore, I commit myself to using my spiritual gifts in a way that builds up the church, fosters unity, and glorifies God, ensuring that my actions reflect the love and wisdom of Christ to those around me.

Reflecting on Mark 16:17, I'm reminded of the significance of tongues as one of the signs that follow those who believe in Christ. Alongside other miraculous signs like healing the sick and casting out demons, speaking in tongues is highlighted as a manifestation of faith and the presence of the Holy Spirit in believers' lives. This passage underscores the ongoing nature of these signs, indicating that they are not limited by time but are intended to accompany believers throughout their journey of faith.

As I delve deeper into the practice of praying or speaking in tongues, I realize its profound importance in my spiritual life. When I engage in this form of prayer, I sense a direct

THE GIFT OF TONGUES

connection with God through the Holy Spirit dwelling within me, reaffirming the truth of John 14:16-17. Unlike other spiritual gifts meant for the edification of the church as a whole, tongues serve as a means for building up my personal faith and spiritual strength.

Moreover, praying or speaking in tongues serves as a gateway to accessing other spiritual gifts and maintaining spiritual purity, as emphasized in passages like 2 Timothy 2:6 and James 3:8. It opens up avenues for prayer beyond my conscious awareness, enabling me to intercede for matters I may not even be cognizant of. This form of prayer requires persistence and sensitivity to the leading of the Holy Spirit, as indicated in Isaiah 28:11-12 and James 5:16.

One of the most profound aspects of praying or speaking in tongues is the realization that it is my spirit communicating directly with God, transcending mere words or thoughts. This intimate connection with the heavenly Father fosters a deeper relationship and prompts me to pray without ceasing, knowing that my spirit is in constant communion with Him. It's a practice that Satan often seeks to hinder, recognizing its potential to strengthen my faith and spiritual vitality.

In essence, praying or speaking in tongues is a sacred gift that not only enriches my prayer life but also deepens my intimacy with God. As I continue to embrace and cultivate this spiritual discipline, I'm confident that it will lead to greater spiritual growth and empowerment in my walk with Christ.

THE GIFT OF
INTERPRETATION OF TONGUES

When I think about the gift of interpreting tongues, I'm reminded of its significance in the context of spiritual communication within the church. This gift allows for the supernatural understanding of messages conveyed through tongues, providing clarity and insight to both the speaker and the listeners.

So, what exactly is the purpose of this remarkable gift? Well, it serves a crucial role in ensuring that the message conveyed through tongues is intelligible and meaningful to those who hear it. As highlighted in 1 Corinthians 14:5, 12, 13, and 16, the goal is to edify both the church and the speaker by bringing forth the message in a way that can be understood and appreciated by all.

THE GIFT OF INTERPRETATION OF TONGUES

Imagine a scenario where someone speaks in tongues during a church gathering. While this act is undoubtedly spiritual and meaningful to the speaker, its impact on others may be limited if no one can comprehend its significance. Here's where the gift of interpretation steps in—it bridges the gap between the spiritual and the practical, making the message accessible to everyone present.

In my own experience, witnessing the gift of interpretation in action has been awe-inspiring. It's like witnessing a divine revelation unfolding before my eyes, as someone receives insight into the hidden meaning behind the tongues spoken. This process not only enriches the spiritual atmosphere of the gathering but also fosters a deeper sense of unity and understanding among believers.

Ultimately, the gift of interpreting tongues is a manifestation of God's grace and wisdom, enabling His message to be communicated effectively within the body of Christ. As I continue to seek spiritual growth and understanding, I'm grateful for the presence of this gift in our midst, knowing that it plays a vital role in edifying and strengthening the church community.

When I think about the difference between translating and interpreting, it's like comparing apples to oranges—they're both related to language, but they serve slightly different purposes.

SPIRITUAL ABUNDANCE

Translating is like taking a text in one language and converting it into another language, usually aiming for a word-for-word or as close to exact meaning as possible. It's like being a linguistic detective, carefully piecing together each word and phrase to ensure that the original message remains intact.

On the other hand, interpreting is more about capturing the essence or overall meaning of a message, rather than focusing on individual words. It's like being a storyteller, summarizing the main points and bringing out the essence of what's being communicated.

So, when it comes to tongues, interpretation is key—it's about uncovering the true meaning behind the spiritual message conveyed, rather than just translating each word. It's about diving deeper into the heart of the message and bringing out its essence in a way that resonates with the listeners.

In my own journey of understanding spiritual gifts, I've come to appreciate the nuanced difference between translation and interpretation. While translation aims for precision, interpretation aims for comprehension, making sure that the message is not just understood, but truly felt and internalized. It's a subtle yet significant distinction that highlights the richness and depth of human communication, both in the natural and the spiritual realms.

Understanding the differences between the gift of prophecy and tongues with interpretation (1 Corinthians 14:1-28) has

THE GIFT OF INTERPRETATION OF TONGUES

been an intriguing journey for me, filled with moments of revelation and deeper insight into the workings of the Holy Spirit in my life.

When I consider the gift of tongues, I see it as a direct line of communication with God, a way to express my prayers, praise, thanksgiving, and exaltation of His name and glory. It's a deeply personal and intimate connection with the divine, where words transcend earthly limitations to reach the heavens. And just as tongues are directed toward God, so too is the gift of interpretation—it's about understanding and conveying the divine messages that flow from the heart of God to His people.

What's fascinating is that the interpretation of tongues isn't received through a sudden burst of revelation, but rather through various means, whether it's pictorial, parabolic, descriptive, or even literal. Sometimes, it comes in the form of a vision, a burden, or a subtle suggestion, unfolding gradually as I open myself to the leading of the Holy Spirit. It's a reminder that God's messages are diverse and can be expressed in myriad ways, tailored to meet the unique needs of His people.

Just like prophecy, the gift of interpretation doesn't override my personality or autonomy. Instead, it's a harmonious collaboration between my spirit and the Holy Spirit, a partnership built on trust and faith. And while all spiritual gifts require faith to operate, I've found that prophecy and revelation demand an extra measure of faith, as they delve into realms beyond the tangible, requiring a deeper surrender to the divine will.

In the end, embracing these gifts isn't just about tapping into their supernatural power—it's about cultivating a deeper relationship with God, allowing His presence to permeate every aspect of my being and ministry. It's a journey of faith, humility, and surrender, where I continually seek His guidance and empowerment to fulfill His purposes in my life and in the lives of those around me.

THE GIFT OF INTERPRETATION OF TONGUES

THE GIFT OF **PROPHECY**

Let's talk about the gift of prophecy—it's definitely not something to be despised. In fact, the Bible explicitly tells us, "Despise not prophesying" (1 Thessalonians 5:20, KJV). This means we shouldn't disregard or look down upon the gift of prophecy when it's exercised in our midst.

Let's dive into what the gift of prophecy really means. For me, prophecy isn't just about predicting the future or speaking in mysterious riddles. It's a powerful form of communication—a vocal miracle, if you will—whereby God inspires someone to speak His truth in their own language. When I prophesy, I do so under the influence of the Holy Spirit, aiming to build up, encourage, and comfort others.

In Hebrew, the word for "prophecy" paints a vivid picture. It's like a bubbling fountain, bursting forth with words from the heart of God. It's as if His message is flowing out freely, like water from a spring. And in Greek, "prophecy" means to speak on behalf of someone else—to be their mouthpiece. So, when I prophesy, I'm essentially speaking for God, conveying His thoughts and intentions to those around me.

It's an incredible responsibility and privilege to be entrusted with such a gift. When I speak as a prophet, I'm not just sharing my own opinions or ideas. Instead, I'm allowing God to use my voice as His instrument, delivering messages of hope, guidance, and truth to His people. And by embracing this role as His mouthpiece, I'm participating in His divine plan to bring light and understanding to those who seek Him.

Think of it this way: Imagine you're at a family gathering, and one of your relatives starts sharing a heartfelt message they feel compelled to deliver. They may not be a professional speaker or have the most polished delivery, but their words are sincere and come from a place of genuine care and concern for everyone present.

Similarly, when someone shares a prophetic word, it may not always be delivered with eloquence or sophistication, but that doesn't diminish its value or significance. The gift of prophecy is a divine communication from God, intended to guide, encourage, and edify His people.

So, instead of dismissing or ridiculing prophetic utterances, we should approach them with humility and an open heart, recognizing that God can speak through anyone, regardless of their background or credentials. When we honor and respect the gift of prophecy, we position ourselves to receive valuable insights and guidance from the Lord for our lives and communities.

Let me clarify what the gift of prophecy is not, drawing from examples in Scripture. First and foremost, it's crucial to understand that prophecy is not synonymous with fortune-telling or divination. In the Bible, we see clear warnings against such practices. Take the example of King Mannaseh, whose actions included engaging in black magic and consulting fortune-tellers. This incurred the wrath of the Lord, as described in 2 Kings 21:6. The passage highlights how the Lord was displeased with Mannaseh's reliance on mediums and wizards, emphasizing the serious nature of such practices.

Similarly, in Jeremiah's time, there were false prophets who claimed to predict the future through dreams and visions. However, God cautioned His people against being deceived by these individuals. He explicitly stated that these prophets prophesied falsely in His name, and He had not sent them. This underscores the importance of discerning true prophecy from false prophecy, as not all who claim to speak for God are genuinely inspired by Him.

These biblical examples serve as a reminder that the gift of prophecy is distinct from fortune-telling or divination. It is a sacred gift bestowed by God for the purpose of edification, exhortation, and comfort within the body of believers. As recipients of this gift, it's essential to use it responsibly and in

THE GIFT OF PROPHECY

alignment with God's will, steering clear of practices that may compromise its integrity or lead others astray.

The gift of prophecy is not dispelling the misconception that it equates to the ability to preach. While preaching involves proclaiming, announcing, and conveying messages, prophecy encompasses something far more profound and supernatural. It's essential to differentiate between the two.

Preaching, as we commonly understand it, often relies on oratorical skills— the ability to captivate an audience through eloquent speech and persuasive delivery. Many individuals, such as politicians, lawyers, and teachers, possess these skills, honed through education and practice, without necessarily being recipients of the Holy Spirit's gift of prophecy. Oratorical ability is primarily a natural talent, accessible to anyone with the inclination and training to develop it.

On the other hand, prophecy transcends mere oratory. It is a supernatural endowment bestowed exclusively by the Holy Spirit. Unlike oratorical ability, which can be acquired through human effort, prophecy is a divine gift that operates beyond the confines of natural talent or training. It originates from the Spirit of God and serves specific purposes within the body of believers. Therefore, it's crucial not to conflate the two, recognizing the distinctiveness of prophecy as a supernatural manifestation of the Spirit.

Let's clear up a common misconception about the gift of prophecy—it's not simply the ability to quote Scripture. While

Scripture quotes may indeed be part of prophecy, it's essential to understand that prophecy goes beyond mere recitation of verses.

Imagine sitting around a campfire with friends, sharing stories and experiences. One friend may have a knack for recalling verses from memory, weaving them seamlessly into conversation. That's a valuable skill, but it doesn't necessarily equate to prophecy. Even the devil himself is known to quote Scripture for his own purposes.

Prophecy, on the other hand, is a spiritual gift, bestowed by the Holy Spirit, that involves speaking forth messages from God. It's not merely regurgitating verses but rather conveying divine insights, revelations, and messages for edification, encouragement, and instruction. While Scripture may serve as a foundation or reference point, prophecy is infused with the power and inspiration of the Holy Spirit, guiding the speaker to communicate God's heart and intentions to His people.

So, let's not confuse the two. While quoting Scripture is valuable, prophecy is a distinct and supernatural gift that operates under the influence and direction of the Holy Spirit, bringing forth messages that go beyond mere words on a page.

Let's set the record straight about the gift of prophecy—it's definitely not about laying empty hands on empty heads. You see, sometimes in certain gatherings or meetings, there are individuals who claim to have the gift of prophecy, but their words don't align with biblical truth. They may make grandiose predictions or declarations that never come to pass, leaving people feeling confused, disappointed, and spiritually wounded.

It's like going to a magic show where the magician promises to make something disappear, but nothing happens. You're left scratching your head, wondering what went wrong. Similarly, when someone claims to prophesy but their words don't bear fruit or bring edification, it's like laying empty hands on empty heads—there's no substance, no genuine connection to the true gift of prophecy as described in the Bible.

True prophecy, as outlined in Scripture, is characterized by accuracy, authenticity, and alignment with God's Word. It's not about empty promises or flimsy predictions that fail to materialize. Instead, it's about speaking forth messages from God that bring clarity, encouragement, and spiritual growth to those who hear them.

So, let's be discerning and cautious when it comes to claims of prophecy. The true gift of prophecy is a powerful and sacred responsibility, not to be taken lightly or misused for personal gain.

Let me share what the gift of prophecy means to me. When I prophesy, I see it as speaking on behalf of God, acting as His mouthpiece to convey His messages to others. It's like I'm entrusted with a sacred task—to deliver His words with clarity and accuracy, guiding His people in the direction He desires.

According to 1 Corinthians 14:29, it's often better to speak in the second or third person when prophesying. This helps ensure that what I say can be easily evaluated and judged by those listening. By speaking in this manner, I'm allowing others to discern the validity and alignment of my words with God's truth.

Additionally, when I step into the role of a prophet, I believe it's important to show reverence to God. That's why I prefer to stand up when I'm prophesying. It's a gesture of honor and respect, acknowledging the divine presence and authority behind the words I speak. Standing in reverence helps me stay connected to God and His will, ensuring that my messages are delivered with humility and sincerity.

THE GIFT OF **KNOWLEDGE**

Let me share what the gift of knowledge means to me. When I receive the WORD OF KNOWLEDGE, it's like getting a direct download of certain facts from the mind of God Himself. It's a supernatural revelation given by His Spirit, revealing things that I couldn't possibly know through natural means alone.

God communicates in various ways, like through dreams, visions, or sometimes even speaking audibly. When I receive this gift, it's as if He's whispering secrets directly to my spirit, guiding me with His divine wisdom and insight.

The gift of knowledge allows me to see beyond the surface—to understand the whereabouts, conditions, or thoughts of people, animals, places, or things. It's like having a glimpse into the heart and mind of others, discerning their deepest secrets and intentions.

THE GIFT OF KNOWLEDGE

This gift isn't just about acquiring information; it's about using it for a greater purpose. I've seen it help in finding lost articles, leading souls to Christ, and even revealing sickness or spiritual oppression in individuals. It's a tool for healing, restoration, and encouragement, building up faith and bringing people closer to God.

Through the gift of knowledge, I'm reminded of the supernatural presence and power of God in my life. It's a humbling experience to be entrusted with such insights, knowing that it's not about my abilities but about His grace working through me to impact the lives of others.

When I talk about the Gift of Knowledge, I'm not referring to the kind of knowledge you gain from textbooks or classrooms. It's not education or simply teaching what you've learned through studying. This gift goes beyond mere human understanding—it's a supernatural insight given by the Holy Spirit.

You see, it's not like psychology or any other science of the mind. Those fields can be practiced by anyone, whether they have the Holy Spirit or not. But the Gift of Knowledge is different. It's a spiritual gift bestowed upon believers by God Himself.

When I receive this gift, it's like tapping into a higher wisdom, one that surpasses human intellect. It's about gaining insights that go beyond what can be learned through natural

SPIRITUAL ABUNDANCE

means. It's about understanding things on a deeper, more spiritual level.

The Gift of Knowledge isn't about acquiring information for the sake of knowledge itself. Instead, it's about using that knowledge to serve a greater purpose—to help others, to bring healing, to provide guidance, and to glorify God. It's a gift that empowers me to see beyond the surface and discern things with spiritual clarity.

So, when I talk about the Gift of Knowledge, I'm talking about something far more profound than just knowing facts or figures. It's about receiving divine revelation and using it to make a difference in the lives of those around me.

When I talk about the Gift of Knowledge, I want to make it clear that it's not about fortune telling. God's Word condemns fortune telling as being of the devil, and I fully believe that. You see, the devil is clever—he tries to counterfeit God's gifts, making it seem like fortune telling is the same as the word of knowledge. But there's a big difference.

When someone claims to have supernatural knowledge through fortune telling, it's not coming from the Holy Spirit. It's not the kind of knowledge that God gives through His gifts. Instead, it's often used to instill fear, confusion, and chaos. The devil uses fortune tellers to bring about harm—to disrupt lives, break hearts, and create chaos.

But when God bestows the Gift of Knowledge, it's for a completely different purpose. He gives this gift to build up His

THE GIFT OF KNOWLEDGE

people, to strengthen them, and to guide them. It's about bringing hope, healing, and restoration—not fear and destruction. When I receive the Gift of Knowledge, I know that it's from God, and it's meant to bring blessing, not harm.

So, let's be clear: the Gift of Knowledge is not about predicting the future or gaining insight through fortune telling. It's about receiving divine wisdom from God Himself, for the purpose of uplifting and edifying His people.

The Gift of Knowledge is not about having all the knowledge in the world. It's not like God just hands us a big book of everything there is to know. Instead, it's about receiving a specific word or piece of knowledge from the Holy Spirit.

God doesn't reveal all His knowledge to us at once. Instead, He gives us glimpses, insights, and understanding as He sees fit. It's like receiving a puzzle piece—a part of the whole picture. And just like a puzzle, over time, those pieces start to come together to reveal a bigger picture.

Now, I'm not saying that God won't reveal more to us in the future. In fact, the Bible tells us that one day, in the perfect age, we will know Him fully, just as He knows us. But for now, we receive these words of knowledge from God as a gift to help us grow in understanding and faith.

The Gift of Knowledge is not just about making educated guesses or relying on our imagination. It's not like solving a puzzle with our intellect or mind. Instead, it's about something deeper—it's about a direct communication from God to our spirit.

This gift doesn't operate through our natural thinking process or our mental abilities. It's not about using our brains to figure things out. Instead, it's a spiritual experience where God speaks directly to our inner being, bypassing our rational thought process.

Imagine it like receiving a sudden insight or intuition—a knowing that comes from deep within. It's not something we can explain or reason out; it's just a sense of understanding that we receive from God Himself. It's like a light bulb moment when everything suddenly clicks into place, and we just know it in our spirit.

The Gift of Knowledge, is not just about having knowledge about God or His Word. Sure, we can gain knowledge through learning, studying, and even through our own life experiences. Take Eli, the priest, for example. He had a wealth of knowledge about God and His Word, accumulated over years of service and experience in the temple.

But here's the thing: the Gift of Knowledge goes beyond what we can learn through conventional means. It's not about academic knowledge or intellectual understanding. It's about receiving insights and revelations directly from God Himself, through the Holy Spirit.

Consider the story of young Samuel, who didn't have Eli's years of experience or knowledge. Despite his lack of formal

THE GIFT OF KNOWLEDGE

education or training, Samuel received a direct word from God while he was still a child. It shows that this gift isn't dependent on human learning or expertise—it's about God choosing to reveal His truths to us in a supernatural way.

So, while knowledge about God and His Word is valuable and important, the Gift of Knowledge operates on a different level—it's about receiving divine insights and revelations that go beyond what we could ever learn on our own.

The Gift of Knowledge, is not primarily about speaking—it's about knowing. This gift doesn't manifest through vocal expression but through inner understanding and insight.

For example, if the Lord imparts a word of knowledge to me, it's not my role to immediately speak it out like a preacher or a teacher would. Instead, it's about receiving that knowledge internally and allowing it to guide my actions or decisions.

Speaking out a word of knowledge is more aligned with other forms of ministry, such as teaching, exhortation, or preaching. In those cases, the knowledge received from the Lord might be shared verbally to encourage or instruct others. But the essence of the Gift of Knowledge lies in the inner knowing and understanding that comes directly from the Holy Spirit.

The Gift of Knowledge plays a crucial role in various aspects of my life and ministry. One area where it's especially needed is in counseling sessions. When someone comes to me with a problem or a struggle, having the gift of knowledge allows me to discern the root issues and provide guidance or support accordingly.

In evangelism, this gift is invaluable. Whether I'm sharing the Gospel with someone one-on-one or preaching to a larger audience, the Holy Spirit can give me insights or words of knowledge about the person or situation, helping me communicate effectively and minister to their specific needs.

Intercession is another area where the Gift of Knowledge comes into play. Sometimes, I'll sense a prompting from the Holy Spirit to pray for someone, even if I don't know the details of their situation. This gift enables me to pray with greater discernment and effectiveness, lifting up specific needs or concerns that I might not be aware of otherwise.

When it comes to giving, the Gift of Knowledge helps me discern when and how to be generous. Whether it's giving financially, offering my time and resources, or extending a helping hand, this gift guides me in being a good steward of what I have and blessing others as a result.

In spiritual warfare, the Gift of Knowledge is like a strategic advantage. It allows me to understand the schemes and tactics of the enemy, discerning when and where he's active so that I can stand firm and pray with authority against his attacks.

Moreover, this gift enables me to be a source of encouragement to others. Sometimes, people may be struggling silently, and I might not be aware of their

THE GIFT OF KNOWLEDGE

difficulties. But with the Gift of Knowledge, the Holy Spirit can reveal to me when someone needs a word of encouragement or affirmation, allowing me to uplift and support them in their journey.

Lastly, the Gift of Knowledge also empowers me to address issues that need correction or rebuke. By discerning the root causes of certain behaviors or attitudes, I can lovingly confront them and help bring about healing and growth in those areas.

THE GIFT OF **WISDOM**

The Gift of Wisdom is like having a divine compass that guides me through life's complexities. It's not just about having knowledge; it's about knowing how to apply that knowledge with insight and discernment. When I encounter challenges or dilemmas, this gift enables me to see beyond the surface and understand the deeper significance of the situation.

God doesn't just provide knowledge; He also gives wisdom on the what, why, where, when, and how of a problem. It's like receiving divine illumination that sheds light on the best course of action. Whether it's navigating a personal crisis, resolving a conflict, or making a decision, the Gift of Wisdom offers supernatural guidance.

In essence, this gift is a supernatural solution to trouble. It's not about relying solely on my own understanding or expertise but on God's wisdom working through me. It's about tapping

THE GIFT OF WISDOM

into the infinite wisdom of heaven to address the challenges I face in my everyday life.

This ability is bestowed upon me by the Holy Spirit, who reveals what to do in various situations. Whether I'm a mother managing a household, a pastor shepherding a congregation, or a business owner serving customers, the Gift of Wisdom equips me to make wise decisions tailored to the specific needs and circumstances.

For example, as a mother, I may encounter different parenting challenges with each of my children, requiring me to apply wisdom and discernment in unique ways. Similarly, as a pastor or church leader, I need to understand the individual needs and struggles of each member of my congregation, guiding them with wisdom and compassion. And as a merchant, I must adapt my approach to meet the diverse needs and preferences of my customers, using discernment to provide excellent service.

Overall, the Gift of Wisdom is an invaluable tool that empowers me to navigate life's complexities with divine insight and understanding. It's a gift that I rely on daily, trusting in God's wisdom to guide me in every situation I encounter.

The Gift of Wisdom is like a special light that shines from above, guiding me through life's twists and turns. It's not something I can acquire through traditional learning or earthly methods. While education and training have their place, they can't compare to the divine wisdom imparted by the Holy Spirit.

I've learned that relying solely on my own understanding or worldly wisdom can lead to mixed results. Sure, some methods may seem effective in certain situations, but they can also backfire unexpectedly. What works beautifully in one scenario may prove ineffective or even harmful in another, especially in the context of church life.

Without the guidance of the Holy Spirit, I'm like a ship navigating treacherous waters without a compass. I may stumble upon solutions by trial and error, but true wisdom comes from above. It's a gift that transcends human knowledge and understanding, offering divine insight into life's complexities.

For instance, as I lead and serve in my church community, I've encountered numerous challenges that required wisdom beyond my own capabilities. Whether it's resolving conflicts, making decisions, or offering counsel, I've come to rely on the wisdom that comes from God's Spirit.

In those moments, I've discovered that the Gift of Wisdom enables me to see beyond the surface and discern the best course of action. It's like having a supernatural guide by my side, helping me navigate through the complexities of ministry and relationships with clarity and discernment.

So, while earthly knowledge and methods have their place, they pale in comparison to the wisdom that comes from God.

THE GIFT OF WISDOM

It's a wisdom that surpasses human understanding and equips me to face life's challenges with confidence and grace.

The Gift of Wisdom isn't just about having deep spiritual insights or understanding Scripture. It's not something I can achieve through years of studying the Bible or being spiritually mature. While those things are important, they don't necessarily mean I possess this supernatural gift.

The Gift of Wisdom are bestowed by the Holy Spirit as He sees fit. It is not something I can earn or acquire through my own efforts. Instead, they're manifestations of the Spirit's power and presence in my life, given for the benefit of the church and the glory of God.

So, while I may strive to deepen my understanding of God's Word and cultivate spiritual maturity, the Gift of Wisdom is ultimately a divine gift that comes from God Himself. It's His way of equipping me to navigate life's complexities with discernment and clarity, empowering me to make wise decisions and offer sound counsel to others as He leads.

The Gift of Wisdom isn't about understanding human behaviour through psychology or studying the natural ways of people. It's not something I can gain from textbooks or lectures in a classroom, delving into the complexities of the human mind. No, this gift goes far beyond earthly wisdom and knowledge.

For me, it's been crucial to understand that the Gift of Wisdom is supernatural in nature. It's a divine endowment, bestowed upon me by the Holy Spirit for a specific purpose. Unlike psychology, which focuses on understanding human behaviour through observation and analysis, this gift operates on a higher plane, tapping into God's wisdom and insight.

While psychology may offer valuable insights into human behaviour and thought patterns, the Gift of Wisdom goes beyond the limitations of human understanding. It's about receiving divine revelation and discernment from God Himself, enabling me to see situations and people through His eyes and respond accordingly.

So, as I seek to grow in wisdom, I recognize that it's not about acquiring knowledge from earthly sources but about opening myself up to the supernatural wisdom of God. It's about trusting in His guidance and allowing His Spirit to lead me in all aspects of life, knowing that His wisdom far surpasses anything I could ever learn on my own.

The Gift of Wisdom isn't just about having simple wisdom gained from reading the Bible or studying God's Word. While that's important for every Christian, this gift goes deeper. Take Solomon, for example; he was known for his wisdom, granted by God. But even he received specific words of wisdom or revelations only occasionally, for particular challenges he faced. Similarly, as a young believer, I might possess the Gift of Wisdom without having extensive Biblical knowledge due to my spiritual immaturity.

THE GIFT OF WISDOM

Moreover, it's essential to understand that the Gift of Wisdom isn't about having access to all of God's wisdom. It's about receiving a specific word or insight from Him for a particular situation or problem. God doesn't reveal His entire storehouse of wisdom to us; instead, He gives us what we need when we need it, through His Spirit.

Another misconception is that this gift is reserved for preachers or church officials. In reality, it's available to all who have received the Holy Spirit. Whenever I face a challenge or dilemma beyond my own understanding, I can rely on the Holy Spirit to impart His wisdom to me through this gift.

It is crucial to recognize that the Gift of Wisdom isn't just about having a random idea or guess that pops into my head. It's not a product of human thought or reasoning. Even non-believers can stumble upon new insights or ideas, but this gift operates on a supernatural level, facilitated by the Holy Spirit's presence within me.

The Gift of Wisdom often comes to me through various means, such as visions, dreams, revelations, a still small voice, or even an audible voice. Just as God speaks to individuals in different ways, the manifestations of this gift can vary greatly. Sometimes, it's a vivid dream that provides clarity and guidance, while other times, it's a gentle whisper in my spirit directing me towards the right path.

I've experienced moments where a vision suddenly illuminates my mind, revealing insights and solutions that were previously hidden. These visions can be like a light breaking through the darkness, showing me the way forward in challenging situations. Similarly, God has spoken to me through dreams, using symbols and imagery to convey profound truths or specific instructions.

Revelations are another powerful channel through which the Gift of Wisdom operates. In moments of prayer or meditation, God unveils deeper understanding and knowledge, unraveling mysteries and revealing His plans. His still small voice, though subtle, carries immense wisdom, guiding me with gentle nudges and promptings along my journey.

And then, there are those rare occasions when I hear an audible voice, unmistakably divine, speaking words of wisdom and counsel. These moments are like encounters with the Almighty, leaving an indelible mark on my heart and mind.

Indeed, God's communication is multifaceted, and the Gift of Wisdom manifests itself through these diverse means, each tailored to meet my specific needs and circumstances. As I continue to seek His guidance and listen for His voice, I trust that He will continue to impart His wisdom to me in ways that are beyond my comprehension.

THE GIFT OF WISDOM

THE GIFT OF **DISCERNING OF SPIRITS**

The Gift of Discerning of Spirits is like having spiritual radar that allows me to perceive the nature of the spiritual realm around me. It's God's Spirit informing my spirit-filled heart about the type of spirit that is being manifested in a particular situation. It's a supernatural insight into the spiritual world, offering clarity amidst the unseen forces at work.

With this gift, I can discern whether a spiritual manifestation is from God, the devil, man, or the world. It's not about mind reading, psychic abilities, or finding fault with others. Instead, it's about being attuned to the Holy Spirit's leading and discerning His presence in any given circumstance.

THE GIFT OF DISCERNING OF SPIRITS

The discerning of spirits is a partnership between me and the Holy Spirit. He bears witness with my spirit, confirming whether something is aligned with God's will or not. It's a profound connection that empowers me to navigate the spiritual landscape with wisdom and insight.

This gift enables me to detect the realm of spirits and their activities. Whether it's unclean spirits, demonic forces, or the Holy Spirit Himself, I can discern their presence and influence. It's like having a spiritual X-ray vision that reveals the plans and purposes of the enemy and guards against spiritual attacks.

In ministries like deliverance and prophecy, the Gift of Discerning of Spirits is indispensable. It ensures that I can accurately identify and address demonic presence and false prophecies. Without it, I'd be left guessing, unable to effectively minister to those in need or judge the authenticity of spiritual manifestations.

Ultimately, this gift is a safeguard for the church, protecting it from the infiltration of demonic influences and practices. By discerning spirits, I contribute to the spiritual safety and well-being of the body of Christ, ensuring that it remains grounded in God's truth and protected from spiritual harm.

The Gift of Discerning of Spirits is definitely not about being suspicious of others. It's not just about having a skeptical mindset or constantly questioning people's motives. Even those who haven't experienced the Holy Spirit can be suspicious of everyone they encounter, but that's not what this gift is about.

It's also important to understand that this gift isn't about criticizing or finding fault with others. It's not about nitpicking or pointing out flaws in people's behavior or character. Instead, it's about discerning the spiritual forces at work behind the scenes, whether they're of God or of the enemy.

Furthermore, it's not just about having a general sense of discernment. While anyone can discern different colors, shapes, and sizes of things, the Gift of Discerning of Spirits goes beyond that. It's a supernatural ability given by God to discern the spiritual realm, to see beyond the physical and into the spiritual dimensions.

And let's be clear: this gift has nothing to do with spiritism, which is condemned in the Scriptures. Spiritism involves communication with the spirits of the dead, which is not what the Gift of Discerning of Spirits is about. Instead, it's about discerning the presence and activity of spiritual forces, whether they're demonic or divine.

As the influence of spiritism and demonic activity increases in the world, the need for the Gift of Discerning of Spirits becomes more crucial than ever. It's a gift that helps us navigate the spiritual landscape with wisdom and clarity, protecting us from deceptive influences and guiding us in God's truth.

THE GIFT OF DISCERNING OF SPIRITS

The Gift of Discerning of Spirits plays a crucial role in prophecy, especially when it comes to judging the authenticity of prophetic messages. It helps me distinguish between spirits, enabling me to discern whether a prophecy is truly from God or not. This gift becomes particularly important in evaluating prophecies that may contain scriptures but still be inaccurate or misleading.

Moreover, the Gift of Discerning of Spirits operates in various aspects of spiritual ministry, including recognizing the work of the enemy, facilitating healing, performing miracles, aiding in deliverance, and identifying false teachers. It allows me to perceive the spiritual forces at play in these situations and discern their true nature.

In my journey of discernment, I've learned to recognize three major types of spirits: the Spirit of God, the human spirit, and demonic spirits. Each of these spirits manifests differently, and the gift helps me discern their presence and influence in different contexts.

To effectively discern spirits, I've become familiar with various types of spirits that may be encountered in spiritual warfare and ministry. These include foul spirits, religious spirits, spirits of lust, adultery, homosexuality, and many others. By understanding and identifying these spirits, I can better navigate the spiritual realm and fulfill my role as a discerner of spirits.

So, what exactly is spiritual discernment? For me, it's about seeking guidance from the Holy Spirit when facing decisions or uncertainties in life. It's like asking for a divine compass to navigate through the complexities of existence. Through spiritual discernment, the Spirit reveals God's will for the church and its people, guiding us toward what God desires us to do and become.

Discernment covers a wide range of areas, including identifying spiritual gifts, discerning spirits, understanding the motivations behind actions, and recognizing the prevailing spiritual atmosphere of our times. It's about seeing beyond the surface and understanding the deeper spiritual realities at play.

I've come to understand that discernment is more than just a skill—it's a gift bestowed by God. However, like any skill, it can be honed and developed through training and experience. As I've journeyed through life, I've learned to rely on the Holy Spirit's guidance more and more, trusting that He will illuminate my path and reveal God's purposes to me.

When the Spirit is moving, there are telltale signs: a deep commitment to Christ-centered spirituality, a rejection of prejudice and exclusivity, a fervent focus on worshipping Jesus, and an extraordinary level of passion and impact in ministry.

In discerning spiritual matters, there are key criteria to consider. Firstly, discernment should always be motivated by love, as anything done without love is futile. It should also

THE GIFT OF DISCERNING OF SPIRITS

center on Jesus Christ and His gospel, leading us closer to Him and His teachings.

Additionally, true discernment aligns with Scripture, never contradicting its principles but rather illuminating them. Moreover, it should edify the church and its members, empowering them with wisdom, character, and unity.

Lastly, genuine discernment fosters a love for righteousness, a recognition of sin, and a turning away from evil, cultivating a life of holiness and purity.

THE GIFT OF **FAITH**

So, what exactly is the gift of faith? For me, it's that remarkable ability given by God to believe in the seemingly impossible and to see it come to fruition through my words and actions. Moreover, it's about imparting that same unwavering faith to others, inspiring them to believe for the extraordinary.

The gift of faith isn't just your everyday, run-of-the-mill belief. It's not the kind of faith we rely on to get through our daily routines or face life's challenges. No, this is something different—it's supernatural, beyond the realms of ordinary human faith.

Now, when we talk about faith, it's essential to understand that there are different types. First, there's saving faith—the faith we exercise when we accept Christ as our Savior. Then there's the fruit of faith, which blossoms in our lives after we've experienced salvation. And finally, there's the gift of faith, a

THE GIFT OF FAITH

special endowment from God that typically manifests after receiving the baptism in the Holy Spirit.

Jesus Himself spoke about this unique kind of faith, urging us to have faith in God—not just any faith, but the supernatural gift of faith that moves mountains and defies the odds.

Now, let's delve into the nature of this gift. The Greek word for faith, "pistis," conveys a deep conviction and reliance, not merely a superficial belief. It's about placing absolute trust in God's promises and power.

It's crucial to distinguish between saving faith and the gift of faith. While salvation comes through faith, the gift of faith is something distinct—a miraculous manifestation of the Spirit that empowers believers to trust God for extraordinary things.

Moreover, the gift of faith is never solitary. It always operates alongside other spiritual gifts, serving as a catalyst for miraculous interventions and divine manifestations.

In operation, the gift of faith is evidenced throughout Scripture, from the accounts of miraculous provisions in the Old Testament to the demonstrations of faith in the New Testament. It's a gift that emboldens believers to step out in audacious trust, confident in God's ability to bring about the impossible.

When it comes to understanding the gift of faith, there are a few things it definitely isn't. First off, it's not simply confidence. Sure, confidence is crucial in many aspects of life, keeping us moving forward even in the face of uncertainty, but it's not quite the same as the supernatural gift of faith. Even those who don't acknowledge the Spirit of God can possess confidence and courage, but the gift of faith is something different—it's a manifestation of the Spirit's power.

Next, let's clarify that the gift of faith isn't synonymous with saving faith. Every Christian needs saving faith to truly embrace Christianity, but the gift of faith goes beyond this foundational belief.

Moreover, it's important to understand that the gift of faith isn't just about hoping something will happen. It's not about wishful thinking or positive affirmations. While hope can certainly motivate us towards our goals, the gift of faith is a divine empowerment, not just a hopeful mindset.

And let's not confuse the gift of faith with theological doctrines or religious practices. It's not about adhering to a set of beliefs or engaging in disciplined prayer routines. While these things are valuable in their own right, they're not the same as the supernatural gift of faith.

Lastly, let's dispel the notion that the gift of faith is a plea for money. It's not about someone standing before a congregation, asking for donations in the name of faith. True faith doesn't hinge on financial demands or materialistic pursuits—it's about trusting in God's provision and stepping out in obedience, regardless of the circumstances.

THE GIFT OF FAITH

THE GIFT OF **WORKING MIRACLES**

When it comes to the spiritual gift of working miracles, it's a powerful display of the Spirit's presence and activity in our lives. Unlike the other spiritual gifts, this one stands out as a supernatural act that defies the laws of nature. It's all about signs and wonders, illustrating the extraordinary power of God at work among us.

Throughout history, we see numerous examples of miracles performed by God's servants to confirm the truth of His Word. These miracles aren't just random acts—they're intentional demonstrations of God's faithfulness and power. They serve to strengthen our faith and build confidence in the message of salvation.

Miracles also play a crucial role in accomplishing God's divine will. They're not just flashy displays of power; they serve specific purposes, such as delivering people from danger, bringing judgment upon those who oppose God's work, and even calming storms or casting out demons. They're God's way of intervening in the natural order of things to bring about His purposes and plans.

Moreover, miracles have a profound impact on people's lives. They can heal broken hearts, set captives free from bondage, and soften stubborn hearts to receive the Holy Spirit. Ultimately, miracles serve as a powerful witness to the reality of God's kingdom and His desire to save and redeem humanity.

So, when we talk about the working of miracles, we're talking about a supernatural power that transcends human ability. It's a tangible expression of God's love and compassion for His creation, and it's a reminder that nothing is impossible for Him.

When it comes to the spiritual gift of working of miracles, it's essential to understand what it's not. First off, it's not about so-called "miracles of science." While advancements in medicine and technology may seem miraculous, they're actually the result of human intellect and natural laws—not the supernatural intervention of God. It's crucial not to confuse human achievements with the manifestation of the Spirit's power.

Similarly, the working of miracles shouldn't be reduced to simply a wonder of nature. While the beauty and complexity of the natural world can inspire awe, true miracles are manifestations of God's power in our lives today. They're not confined to the distant past but are ongoing expressions of God's presence and activity among us.

Furthermore, miracles shouldn't be mistaken for mere surprises. While completing large-scale projects like buildings may seem miraculous in their own right, they're ultimately the result of human effort and ingenuity. Miracles, on the other hand, are supernatural interventions that defy natural explanations and point to the power of God at work.

Lastly, the working of miracles isn't synonymous with modern surgical skills. While surgeons may perform incredible feats in the operating room, their abilities are limited to the natural realm. True miracles go beyond what human hands can achieve and bear witness to the miraculous power of God. They're not dependent on human expertise but on the sovereign intervention of the Spirit.

The Spiritual gift of working of miracles holds a profound purpose in my life. It's like a direct hotline to divine interventions when all other avenues seem closed. When I witness miracles unfolding, it's as if Jesus Himself steps into the scene as the ultimate victor, showing His power over every obstacle and challenge. These miraculous moments are like glimpses of immortality, reminding me of the eternal life that awaits beyond this earthly realm.

Moreover, the gift of working of miracles isn't just about flashy displays of power; it's about meeting real needs in

THE GIFT OF WORKING MIRACLES

tangible ways. Whether it's providing for someone's basic necessities or delivering them from imminent danger, these miracles demonstrate God's unfailing care and provision for His children. They're also a means through which divine judgments are carried out, aligning the course of events with God's ultimate plan and justice.

One of the most profound aspects of this gift is its ability to confirm the Word of God. When miracles occur in conjunction with the preaching of His Word, it's like a stamp of authenticity, validating the truth and authority of Scripture. These divine interventions also serve as powerful testimonies to God's glory, showcasing His majesty and sovereignty in ways that leave us in awe.

And yes, sometimes the working of miracles even includes the seemingly impossible act of raising the dead. In these moments, death itself is defeated, and God's power to bring life out of death is put on full display. It's a reminder that nothing is beyond His reach and that He has the final say over life and death.

Ultimately, the Spiritual gift of working of miracles is a profound expression of God's love, power, and glory. It's a reminder that He is intimately involved in every aspect of our lives, and that nothing is too difficult for Him.

THE GIFTS OF HEALING

The Spiritual gifts of healing hold a special place in my heart, as they embody the miraculous power of God to bring healing and deliverance from all forms of disease and infirmity. Whether it's a functional issue, an organic condition, or a nervous disorder, the healing touch of God knows no bounds. It's like a divine intervention that directly confronts and destroys the work of the devil within the human body, restoring health and wholeness.

What's truly remarkable about the gifts of healing is their versatility. It's not a one-size-fits-all approach; rather, it's like a tailor-made solution for each individual's specific needs. Whether it's physical, emotional, or spiritual healing, God's power knows exactly what's required and provides accordingly. It's like receiving a customized portion of healing grace designed just for me.

THE GIFTS OF HEALING

Moreover, these gifts of healing are not just for personal benefit; they also serve a broader purpose within the church community and beyond. Like tongues, they're given both for individual edification and for the collective strengthening of the church body. It's as if God equips His people with these healing gifts to demonstrate His love and power in a tangible way, both to believers and unbelievers alike.

Indeed, the gifts of healings serve as powerful signs that point to the reality of God's presence and His desire to bring restoration to all aspects of our lives. They're like a beacon of hope, drawing people closer to the truth of the Gospel and opening their hearts to receive the message of salvation. In this way, they play a vital role in fulfilling the Great Commission, empowering evangelists and ministers to proclaim the good news with credibility and authority.

As I reflect on the significance of the gifts of healing, I'm reminded of the miraculous healings recorded in the Bible, where the touch of Jesus brought about instantaneous transformation and healing. Today, that same healing power is available to us through the Holy Spirit, ready to bring wholeness and restoration to all who call upon His name.

The Spiritual gifts of healing are something truly special, something beyond the realm of ordinary medical science or human understanding. It's like tapping into a divine source of power that goes beyond what any textbook or laboratory experiment could ever achieve. While medical science certainly has its place and can do incredible things, the gifts of healing operate on a different level altogether.

It's important to note that the gifts of healing are not to be confused with Christian Science, despite the similarity in name. Christian Science may espouse principles of positivity and mental well-being, but it lacks the foundational truths of Christianity and the supernatural power of God. The gifts of healing operate in the realm of faith and divine intervention, not just positive thinking or mind over matter.

Likewise, the gifts of healing are not to be associated with spiritualism or occult practices. While these may sometimes seem to bring relief or temporary improvement, they ultimately lead to deeper spiritual bondage and suffering. The gifts of healing, on the other hand, come from God and are intended for the restoration and well-being of the individual, both physically and spiritually.

And let's not forget about Extreme Unction, a sacrament practiced by the Roman Catholic Church. While this ritual may have its roots in scripture, it has strayed far from its original intent.

The gifts of healing, as described in the Bible, are about bringing restoration and recovery, not merely preparing someone for death. They are about bringing hope and life, not resignation to fate.

In essence, the gifts of healing are about tapping into the power of God to bring about miraculous transformations in

THE GIFTS OF HEALING

people's lives. They're about restoring health, restoring hope, and restoring faith in the goodness and mercy of God. And that's something truly extraordinary.

The Spiritual gifts of healing are not just about physical restoration; they serve a higher purpose, a divine mission that goes beyond mere bodily health. It's like being part of a grand plan orchestrated by God Himself, where each healing serves a specific purpose in His greater design.

One of the primary purposes of this gift is to demonstrate the reality of Jesus' resurrection and His power to overcome death. When I see someone healed miraculously, it's like a living testimony to the truth of Christ's victory over the grave, just as it was in the days of the early church.

Moreover, the gifts of healing also serve to reveal Jesus' authority to forgive sins. It's not just about physical ailments; it's about spiritual restoration and reconciliation with God. When someone experiences healing, it's a tangible reminder of the forgiveness and grace available through Jesus Christ.

But it doesn't stop there. The gifts of healing are also about building faith and saving souls. When people witness the miraculous works of God, it inspires them to believe in His power and goodness. It's like a beacon of hope drawing lost souls into the loving embrace of their Creator.

Furthermore, these gifts serve to confirm the truth of God's Word. They're like divine endorsements, validating the message preached by His servants. When healing accompanies the proclamation of the gospel, it's like God Himself putting His stamp of approval on His Word.

And let's not forget about the glory of God. Every healing, every miraculous intervention, brings glory and honor to His name. It's a testimony to His goodness, His mercy, and His unfailing love for His children.

Ultimately, the purpose of the gifts of healing is to deliver the sick and destroy the works of the devil. It's about reclaiming what was lost to sin and sickness, restoring wholeness and vitality to body, mind, and spirit.

So, when I think about the gifts of healing, I see them as part of God's master plan to establish His kingdom on earth, to draw people to Himself, and to reveal His glory to the world. And I count it a privilege to be a vessel through which His healing power can flow, bringing joy, wellness, and wholeness to those in need.

FRUIT OF **THE SPIRIT**

The concept of the fruit of the Spirit has always intrigued me—it's like having a single fruit with nine delicious flavors, each one distinct yet complementary. Just like the Mysterio Deliciosus! I often turn to Galatians 5:13-26 to remind myself of these flavors that should be evident in my life as a follower of Christ.

In verses 22-23, Paul beautifully sums up this spiritual fruit basket: love, joy, peace, patience, kindness, goodness, faithfulness, gentleness, and self-control. Each of these flavors represents a characteristic of a true Christian, and they can be grouped into three categories: those relating to God, to others, and to ourselves.

As I reflect on these flavours, I realize that they are not just random traits but essential aspects of my relationship with God and others. Love, joy, and peace speak to my connection with

FRUIT OF THE SPIRIT

God, showing my affection for Him, the joy I find in His presence, and the peace that comes from trusting Him.

The next three flavours—patience, kindness, and goodness—guide my interactions with others. They remind me to be patient in difficult situations, to show kindness to those around me, and to strive for goodness in all my actions.

Finally, the last three flavours—faithfulness, gentleness, and self-control—speak to my personal character and self-discipline. They challenge me to remain faithful to God and His Word, to approach others with gentleness and humility, and to exercise self-control in all aspects of my life.

Overall, I see the fruit of the Spirit as a roadmap for living out my faith in practical ways. Just as a delicious fruit salad combines various flavors to create a harmonious blend, these characteristics work together to shape me into the person God wants me to be.

LOVE

Love as a fruit of the Spirit encompasses a vast spectrum of meanings, and understanding it requires delving into its nuances. In English, we use the word "love" to express a multitude of sentiments. However, in Greek, there are distinct words that capture different aspects of love. There's "storge," which denotes affection, such as the love between a parent and child. Then, there's "phileo," representing friendship, and "eros," signifying romantic and passionate love. C.S. Lewis refers to these three as "natural loves" because they're inherent to human experience, although they can also be corrupted.

But there's another kind of love, one that stands apart from these natural loves – "agape." This is the love that is described as an unconquerable benevolence by William Barclay. It's an active desire and pursuit of the best for others, a deliberate choice rather than a fleeting emotion or reaction. Unlike the

LOVE

natural loves, agape is a matter of the head, not just the heart. It's a love that supplements and complements the natural affections we feel, elevating them to a higher plane.

The Scriptures provide clear guidance on whom we should direct this powerful emotion. First and foremost, I'm called to love God with all my heart, soul, and mind. This love isn't just an option; it's a commandment that permeates every aspect of my life. It's a deep, unwavering affection and devotion that shapes my thoughts, actions, and priorities.

Additionally, I'm reminded to love myself. This isn't about selfishness or arrogance but recognizing my worth and treating myself with kindness and compassion. After all, if I can't love and care for myself, how can I extend genuine love to others?

My love isn't meant to be confined to those who are easy to love or share my beliefs. I'm called to love my neighbors, extending kindness, empathy, and support to those around me, regardless of their background or circumstances. This encompasses not only those in my immediate vicinity but also individuals I encounter in my daily life, whether in person or online.

Moreover, as a member of the body of Christ, I'm instructed to love my brothers and sisters in Christ deeply. This love isn't merely a superficial sentiment but a genuine bond of fellowship and mutual care. It's through this love that we reflect the love of Christ to the world and demonstrate our discipleship.

Perhaps the most challenging aspect of love is extending it to my enemies. Jesus Himself taught us to love our enemies and pray for those who persecute us. This kind of love goes against my natural instincts and requires divine strength and grace. Yet, it's in loving our enemies that we most closely resemble Christ and demonstrate the transformative power of His love.

Ultimately, the question of whom to love is straightforward – everyone. As challenging as it may be at times, I'm called to love unconditionally, without discrimination or reservation. This is the essence of Christ's teachings and the hallmark of a life lived in obedience to Him.

I am learning that it's not about having an agenda or expecting something in return. Love, true love, is unconditional. Jesus Himself exemplified this kind of love in His life and teachings. He laid down His life for us, demonstrating the ultimate sacrifice and selflessness. As I reflect on His example, I realize that love isn't always easy or convenient—it requires genuine care and consideration for others, even when it's challenging.

Sometimes, there are people in my life whom I find it difficult to love. They may have hurt me, betrayed my trust, or simply rubbed me the wrong way. In those moments, I'm reminded to turn to God for help. I ask Him to soften my heart and give me the strength to choose love, even when it's hard. It's a deliberate decision to extend grace and forgiveness, regardless of how I feel.

LOVE

To gauge my capacity for love, I often refer to the checklist found in 1 Corinthians 13. This passage provides a comprehensive guide to what love truly looks like. It challenges me to examine my attitudes, actions, and motives in light of God's standard of love. Do I show patience and kindness to others, or do I harbor resentment and selfishness? Am I quick to forgive, or do I hold onto grudges? These questions help me assess where I stand and identify areas for growth in my love walk.

In my journey of faith, I've come to understand the profound impact that love can have in my relationship with God. He longs for me to know Him intimately, to express my love for Him directly through worship, praise, thanksgiving, and spending time alone with Him. These aspects of my life are crucial for my spiritual growth and connection with the Father, and I'm learning to prioritize them more each day.

It's easy to fall into the trap of relying solely on good works as a means of expressing love to God. However, I've realized that true intimacy with Him goes beyond outward actions. Jesus warned about this in Matthew 7:22-23, emphasizing the importance of spending personal time with God. It's not enough to merely perform deeds; I want to know God deeply, and for Him to know me intimately.

One of the most profound aspects of love is its ability to cast out fear. This truth resonates deeply with me, especially as I've experienced moments of anxiety and uncertainty in my life. 1 John 4:18 reminds me that perfect love drives out all fear. But I've also learned that cultivating this perfect love is an ongoing process. It requires intentional effort to increase my love for the Father, which in turn diminishes fear's hold over my life.

As I continue to grow in love, I'm discovering its transformative power. Love enables me to conquer all things, just as 1 Corinthians 13:8 affirms. I'm reminded that God Himself is love, as stated in 1 John 4:8, and that love is not merely a feeling but a person. Knowing this, I'm inspired to embrace the same spiritual capacity that Jesus demonstrated during His earthly ministry. With love as my guide, I can navigate life's challenges with courage, faith, and unwavering trust in God's unfailing love.

For me, walking in love means surrendering control and allowing the power of God to intervene in the situations I face. As I deepen my fellowship with the Holy Spirit, I've noticed love increasingly manifesting in my life, transforming my attitudes and actions.

Romans 5:5 reminds me that the love of God resides within me, courtesy of the Holy Spirit dwelling in my heart and the presence of Christ's nature within me. This reassures me that love is not just an abstract concept but a tangible reality dwelling within me, ready to be expressed in my interactions with others.

Reflecting on Jesus' prayer in John 17:26, where He prayed for the Father's love for Him to be upon us, fills me with gratitude. It's a profound reminder of the depth of God's love for each of us and His desire for us to experience and express that love in our lives.

The fulfillment of Jesus' prayer is beautifully articulated in 1 John 4:15-16, where I find assurance that I abide in God and He in me because He has given me His Spirit. This truth reinforces my understanding that love is not just a distant ideal but a present reality, empowering me to walk in love daily, just as Jesus did.

Being rooted and grounded in love is crucial, as I've come to realize through Ephesians 3:16-19. Without this foundation, I'm vulnerable to being easily offended, especially when faced with persecution or affliction for the sake of the Word. Reflecting on Mark 4:15-17, I see how responding in the natural realm rather than with the love of God can allow the enemy to steal the Word from my heart.

To become rooted and grounded in love, I've learned two essential practices. Firstly, keeping the Word of God close to my heart, as emphasized in 1 John 2:5, has been instrumental in establishing a strong foundation of love within me. Additionally, I've endeavored to follow God's example, walking in love as Jesus did, as outlined in Ephesians 5:1-2.

Understanding Jesus' example of walking in love has been transformative for me. John 5:17-19 reveals that Jesus did only what the Father did, demonstrating a profound intimacy and alignment with God's will. I've realized that to experience

SPIRITUAL ABUNDANCE

victory in my life, I must emulate Jesus by aligning my actions with the Father's will.

Crucially, I've recognized that cultivating a lifestyle of love requires spending time with the Father. Just as Jesus did, I prioritize developing the fruits of the Spirit by investing significant time in communion with God. Drawing inspiration from Matthew 14:1-14, where Jesus responded with compassion even amidst challenging circumstances, I see the importance of waging spiritual warfare against the enemy's schemes.

Jesus' ability to respond in love, even in the face of adversity, stemmed from His deep connection with the Father. Similarly, I understand that my capacity to walk in love is directly correlated with the time and intimacy I share with God. As I continue to cultivate this relationship and prioritize love in my life, I trust that I'll experience greater victory and resilience in every situation.

LOVE

JOY

Joy is an essential aspect of the Christian life, and it's more than just fleeting happiness. I've come to understand that joy is a powerful spiritual force that emanates from within me as a believer. Unlike happiness, which is often based on external circumstances and fleeting emotions, joy transcends feelings; it's a tangible force that sustains me even in the midst of challenges.

As I delve deeper into the concept of joy, I've realized that it serves as a foundational strength for my spiritual life. In Galatians 5:22-23, joy is listed alongside other fruits of the Spirit, and I've come to see it as the bedrock upon which these other virtues are built. Joy infuses strength into qualities like peace, longsuffering, gentleness, goodness, faith, meekness, and temperance, enabling me to navigate life's ups and downs with resilience.

JOY

Recognizing the significance of joy in my spiritual journey, I've also become aware of the enemy's attempts to counterfeit it through various worldly pleasures. Satan may offer substitutes like drugs, sex, alcohol, or wealth, promising temporary satisfaction, but these pale in comparison to the genuine joy found in Jesus. I've learned that true joy comes from a deep relationship with Him, transcending mere external stimuli and providing a lasting sense of fulfillment and contentment.

Joy is like hitting a slam-dunk in basketball—it's that feeling of pure exhilaration and triumph that comes from deep within. But let's not confuse it with happiness, which is more like scoring a goal in a game—it's great, but it's fleeting and depends on the situation. Sure, being happy is fantastic, but I try not to be a perpetual grinner or walk around looking like I've had a face-off with a rainy day. Happiness is like the weather, always changing with the circumstances, but joy, now that's a whole different ball game.

When I think of joy, I can't help but think of Psalms 30:11 and 1 Thessalonians 1:6. They paint a picture of a joy that's not just a passing feeling but something deeper, something given by the Holy Spirit himself. It's the kind of joy that bubbles up from within, regardless of what's happening on the outside. It's the kind of joy that stays with you even when life throws you a curveball. That's the kind of joy I strive for—a joy that's rooted in God and lasts for eternity.

Joy is more than just a warm, fuzzy feeling—it's essential for me to conquer and overcome in all aspects of my life. When I look at Deuteronomy 28:47-48, I see how the absence of joy led believers to serve the enemy and live under the weight of unfulfilled desires. But on the flip side, serving the Lord with joy and gladness brings victory, fulfillment, and freedom from bondage.

Now, let's talk about the three functions of joy. Firstly, joy produces victory. It's the strength that keeps me steadfast, unmovable, even in the face of trials and tribulations. Just like Jesus, who endured to the point of shedding blood, joy empowers me to overcome every obstacle and endure as a good soldier.

Secondly, joy provides fulfillment. When I cultivate joy in my life, I experience completeness and lack nothing. James 1:2-4 tells me that endurance springs from joy, and Nehemiah 8:10 confirms that joy is the source of strength to endure.

And thirdly, joy protects against opposition. It's the antidote to the yoke of iron that weighs me down in long, drawn-out trials. When joy begins to wither, I know I need to refocus on God and tap into the wellspring of joy that resides in my spirit.

So, joy isn't just about fleeting emotions or temporary circumstances—it's about knowing God and finding contentment in Him. It's about drawing from the bucket of salvation to access all the blessings God has in store for me.

JOY

And most importantly, it's about guarding my heart with joy, even when the storms of life rage around me.

Joy is a fruit that grows within me as my faith develops. There's a beautiful relationship between joy, faith, and the Word of God. When I hear God's Word, my faith is strengthened, and in turn, joy springs up within me. Jesus emphasized this connection when He spoke about the joy that comes from hearing His words, and the apostle John echoed this truth in his writings.

The Old Testament also highlights the link between joy and faith. Passages like Psalm 19:8 and Jeremiah 15:1 illustrate the joy that accompanies a strong faith in God's promises. I've realized that my faith will never surpass the level of my joy, and vice versa—they both rely on the foundation of God's Word.

Seeking God's presence is another key to experiencing joy. As Psalm 16:11 says, in His presence, there is fullness of joy. When I draw near to God with a sincere heart, I find joy that surpasses any sorrow or hardship. But seeking His presence requires me to come with clean hands and a pure heart, willing to examine myself in the light of His Word.

Purifying my heart involves seeking God wholeheartedly, without any ulterior motives. It's about genuinely desiring His presence and being willing to pay the price to dwell in His joy. Jeremiah 29:10-14 reminds me that when I seek God with my whole heart, I will find Him, and with Him, comes overflowing joy.

Just as faith is expressed through words, so is joy. When I speak God's words of joy, it stirs up the joy within me and releases His strength through the Holy Spirit. Additionally, joy is released when I dance before the Lord in worship, as Jeremiah 31:13 describes. And when I pray with faith,

I experience the joy of the Lord welling up inside me, bringing comfort and strength in every situation.

PEACE

Peace isn't just the absence of conflict; it's a profound sense of inner tranquility that can only be found through Jesus Christ. When I gave my life to Him, I received this precious fruit of peace, but like any fruit, it must be cultivated and nurtured. Jesus Himself emphasized the importance of peace, especially in times of trouble, urging us not to be troubled but to trust in Him.

As the world grows increasingly chaotic, with events that would strike fear into the hearts of many, Jesus warns us not to be alarmed. Instead, He encourages us to cultivate peace within ourselves, even amidst the storms of life. This peace isn't just a temporary reprieve from external troubles; it's an inward stability that allows me to face adversity with calm assurance.

One powerful example of this inner peace is found in the story of Daniel in the lion's den. Despite the imminent threat of death, Daniel remained serene and untroubled, able to rest peacefully even in the midst of danger. This kind of peace goes beyond mere circumstances; it's a deep-seated confidence in God's presence and protection, even when everything around us seems to be falling apart.

Ultimately, the source of this peace is the sacrificial blood of Jesus Christ. His death on the cross paved the way for us to experience true peace, not just fleeting moments of calm, but a lasting, unshakeable assurance that transcends any earthly turmoil. As I continue to walk with Him and abide in His love, I find that His peace becomes a steadfast anchor in the storms of life, allowing me to rest securely in His promises.

Peace isn't just a passive state of calm; it's a powerful force that actively guards our hearts and minds against the attacks of the enemy. When I pray and cast my cares upon the Lord, His peace acts like a vigilant army, protecting me from the onslaught of worry and fear. But too often, I've found myself letting down my guard, allowing anxious thoughts to take control and drowning out God's voice.

Just like Martha in the Bible, I've sometimes prioritized busyness over intimacy with God, substituting serving for sitting at His feet. But Jesus gently reminds me, as He did Martha, that the most important thing is to choose the one thing that is needful—to abide in His presence and receive His peace. When I allow God's peace to rule in my heart, it becomes like an umpire, guiding me in the right direction and helping me discern His will.

One of the most beautiful aspects of peace is its ability to transform us into peacemakers. As I cultivate the fruit of peace in my own heart, it naturally overflows to those around me, just as Jesus, the Prince of Peace, ministered peace to others during His earthly ministry. Being a peacemaker isn't just about avoiding conflict; it's about actively pursuing reconciliation and forgiveness, just as Christ did for me.

In moments of tension or conflict, I've learned to let the fruit of peace guide my words and actions, choosing to respond with gentleness and grace rather than reacting in anger or frustration.

As Proverbs 15:1 reminds me, a soft answer can turn away wrath and diffuse volatile situations. By following the example of Jesus and allowing His peace to reign in my heart, I can live a life characterized by harmony and reconciliation, reflecting the love and forgiveness of the Prince of Peace Himself.

Developing and cultivating peace in my life begins with prayer. When I pray, I'm not just presenting my requests to God; I'm also expressing my faith and gratitude. As Philippians 4:6-7 reminds me, prayer accompanied by thanksgiving is like fertile soil for the fruit of peace to grow. Even in the midst of challenges, offering prayers filled with gratitude and praise can usher in a sense of peace that surpasses understanding.

Abiding in Jesus is another key to cultivating peace. Isaiah 26:3 assures me that as I keep my focus on God, He will envelop me in His perfect peace. Just as a branch draws

PEACE

nourishment and strength from the vine, so I find peace and security by remaining connected to Jesus, the source of all peace. In John 15:4-5, Jesus Himself assures me that abiding in Him results in bearing the fruit of peace.

Keeping God's Word close to my heart is essential for cultivating lasting peace. Psalm 119:165 emphasizes that loving and obeying God's Word leads to a deep sense of peace. When I align my life with His truth and follow His commands, I experience the peace that comes from living in harmony with His will. Philippians 4:9 encourages me to let the peace of God flow freely in my life by meditating on His Word and putting it into practice.

Ultimately, cultivating peace requires a lifestyle of surrender and obedience to God's will. As I commit to prayer, abiding in Jesus, and cherishing His Word, I create fertile ground for the fruit of peace to flourish in my life. In every situation, whether in times of trial or triumph, I can trust that the peace of God will guard my heart and mind, providing security and serenity that can only be found in Him.

We are assured of peace in various aspects of our lives, from the sanctuary of God's house to the expanses of eternity. In 1 Kings 22:17, I find peace in the presence of the Lord, knowing that His house is a sanctuary of tranquility. Leviticus 26:6 promises peace within the land, a reassurance of security and serenity. Even in the face of death, as mentioned in 2 Kings 22:20, I can find peace knowing that God's peace transcends even the grave.

SPIRITUAL ABUNDANCE

Prosperity is not devoid of peace, as 1 Samuel 25:6 assures me that abundance is accompanied by peace. And when everything culminates in the end, Psalm 37:37 promises that peace will be my portion. In the depths of my mind, Philippians 4:7 assures me that God's peace will guard my thoughts and emotions, providing a sense of calm amidst life's storms.

As a believer, I can experience various dimensions of God's peace. Isaiah 26:3 describes it as perfect peace, a deep-seated assurance that comes from trusting in the Lord. Psalm 119:165 speaks of great peace that envelops those who love God's law, a peace that transcends understanding. Through 2 Peter 1:2, I discover that peace can be multiplied in my life, overflowing in abundance.

God's peace extends beyond external circumstances to the very depths of my being. Psalm 122:8 assures me of peace within, a tranquility that comes from being in harmony with God's will. Proverbs 16:7 promises peace even in the presence of enemies, while 2 Thessalonians 5:13 encourages peace among brethren. Romans 5:1 declares that through Christ, I have peace with God, reconciled and restored to Him.

Philippians 4:7 reminds me that God's peace surpasses understanding, guarding my heart and mind in Christ Jesus. As a believer, I am called to live in peace (2 Corinthians 13:11), to lie down and sleep in peace (Psalm 4:8), and to sow seeds of peace wherever I go (James 3:18). Hebrews 12:14 urges me to pursue peace with all people, reflecting the peace that Christ brings.

PEACE

In every aspect of my life, whether in my comings and goings, my interactions with others, or my proclamation of the Gospel, peace is both my companion and my garment (Ephesians 6:15). As I walk in the footsteps of peace, I embody the message of reconciliation and harmony that Christ brought to the world.

LONGSUFFERING

Longsuffering is more than just a word; it's a quality I need to embody when I have the Holy Spirit dwelling within me. If He's going to be my closest companion, then I must bear His fruit—the very essence of His character. Longsuffering, in simple terms, means enduring hardship with patience, remaining steadfast even in the face of adversity. It's a trait that reflects God's own nature, as seen in passages like Exodus 34:6 and 1 Timothy 1:16. Interestingly, its purpose isn't just to test us but to lead us toward repentance, as mentioned in Romans 2:4.

As I dive into the Scriptures, I notice various words used to convey the essence of longsuffering. It's not just about patience but also about perseverance, forbearance, tolerance, and endurance. These different expressions in the Bible highlight the multifaceted nature of this fruit of the Spirit. In

LONGSUFFERING

Greek, three distinct words capture the essence of longsuffering: "anecho," which implies holding up under pressure or bearing with; "hupomone," indicating enduring under trial or persevering; and "makrothumi," meaning being slow to anger or patiently enduring.

Each of these Greek terms paints a unique aspect of longsuffering, showcasing its depth and breadth. From bearing with others' shortcomings to enduring trials with patience, longsuffering encompasses a range of experiences. It's about remaining steadfast in love, even when provoked or faced with difficult circumstances. As I navigate life's challenges, I'm reminded of the importance of embodying the qualities encapsulated in longsuffering—tolerance, endurance, and a patient spirit.

Longsuffering isn't just a passive acceptance of adversity; it's an active choice to remain rooted in faith and love despite the storms of life. It's about extending grace and understanding to others, just as God has shown me. As I strive to cultivate longsuffering in my life, I draw strength from the knowledge that God Himself embodies this trait. With His Spirit dwelling within me, I can face life's trials with a spirit of endurance, knowing that His grace is more than sufficient to sustain me.

God's longsuffering or patience is truly remarkable—it's a quality I often find myself reflecting on in awe. Despite all the flaws and failings of humanity, He remains steadfastly patient, waiting for just the right moment to intervene. He could have

SPIRITUAL ABUNDANCE

easily resolved all the world's problems long ago, but His patience extends far beyond what we can comprehend.

Longsuffering, however, isn't just about enduring hardships; it's rooted in love—for God and for others. As I reflect on 1 Corinthians 13:4, I'm reminded that patience is an integral part of love. It's not merely a matter of exercising self-control, although that certainly plays a role. Instead, it flows from my relationship with Christ. Jesus himself emphasized this connection when He spoke about being the vine and us being the branches. He stressed the importance of remaining in Him to bear fruit, emphasizing the command to love one another.

In the same passage from John, Jesus also talks about the pruning of the branches by the Father. This pruning, or discipline, is essential for our growth and fruitfulness. While it may come in the form of trials and testing, its purpose is to refine us, making us more fruitful in our love and service to others. Hebrews 12:11 speaks to this process, highlighting how discipline ultimately leads to a harvest of righteousness and peace for those who embrace it.

Understanding God's patience and the purpose of longsuffering in my life helps me navigate the challenges and trials that come my way. Instead of seeing them as obstacles, I can view them as opportunities for growth and refinement. Just as a gardener carefully tends to his plants, so does God lovingly discipline me, shaping me into the person He intends me to be.

LONGSUFFERING

And through it all, His patience serves as a beacon of hope, reminding me of His unwavering love and faithfulness.

Longsuffering is essential for enduring the challenges of life—it's like the fuel that keeps us going in the marathon race of faith. When I think about the examples of endurance in the Bible, I'm inspired by the steadfastness of figures like Paul, who faced countless trials and hardships yet never wavered in his commitment to the finish line. His determination to press on, even in the face of adversity, serves as a powerful reminder of the importance of longsuffering in our journey of faith.

In addition to producing endurance, longsuffering also fosters unity among believers. Forgiveness and patience go hand in hand, allowing us to overlook each other's faults and extend grace just as we have received it from God. I'm reminded of the parable Jesus told about the servant who was forgiven a massive debt but refused to show the same mercy to others. It's a sobering reminder that without longsuffering, strife and unforgiveness can easily take root in our relationships.

Cultivating longsuffering requires intentional effort—it's not something that happens automatically. Just as we "put on" clothing, we must actively choose to develop this fruit of the Spirit in our lives. This means practicing forbearance and forgiveness, even when it's difficult. As James warns in his epistle, failing to be longsuffering with one another can lead to destruction within the body of believers.

Moreover, longsuffering enables us to obtain the promises of God. The examples of Abraham, Caleb, and Noah demonstrate the rewards of patient endurance. Their steadfastness in waiting for God's promises to be fulfilled serves as a testament to the power of longsuffering in obtaining blessings from the Lord. Yet, many of us fall short in this area because we lack the patience and endurance required to stand firm in our faith.

Ultimately, longsuffering is about persevering in faith and love, even when faced with challenges and obstacles. It's a quality that enables us to endure trials, foster unity, and obtain the promises of God. As I strive to cultivate longsuffering in my own life, I'm reminded of the importance of standing firm in faith, trusting that God's timing is perfect and His promises are true.

Cultivating longsuffering requires intentional effort and a willingness to align our hearts with God's Word. One way to cultivate this fruit is by diligently keeping the Word of God in our hearts and obeying it wholeheartedly. Just as Jesus taught in the parable of the sower, when we receive the Word with a steadfast heart, it takes root and produces fruit in our lives.

Another avenue for cultivating longsuffering is through experiencing tribulations. While facing trials may not seem pleasant, they provide an opportunity for growth and endurance. Instead of allowing trials to overwhelm us with worry and doubt, we can choose to wait on God with hopeful expectation, knowing that He is faithful to see us through every

LONGSUFFERING

trial. As Isaiah 40:31 reminds us, those who wait upon the Lord will renew their strength and soar on wings like eagles.

Maintaining hope is crucial for cultivating longsuffering in our lives. Just as Abraham held onto hope in the face of seemingly impossible circumstances, we too can anchor our hope in the promises of God. By focusing on what God has said about our situation, keeping our eyes fixed on His Word, and rejecting doubts and unbelief, we can cultivate a spirit of longsuffering that enables us to endure trials with patience and perseverance.

MEEKNESS or KINDNESS

Meekness isn't weakness; it's a strength of character that's rooted in self-control. When I'm meek, I'm slow to take offense, even in the face of unjust treatment or persecution for the sake of the gospel. It's about exercising self-control and remaining steadfast in the midst of adversity, rather than reacting impulsively or retaliating against those who wrong me. In essence, self-control is a key aspect of meekness, allowing me to respond with grace and patience, even when faced with challenging circumstances.

Consider the story of Moses in Numbers 12:1-13. Despite being unjustly criticized by his own brother and sister, Moses displayed remarkable meekness. Instead of defending himself, he remained silent and allowed God to defend him. This act of meekness not only demonstrated Moses' strength of character but also his humility and reliance on God in the face of opposition.

Meekness empowers me to respond to criticism and adversity with intercession rather than retaliation. In 2 Timothy 2:24-26, Paul emphasizes the importance of meekness in responding to those who oppose the truth. By approaching others with meekness and humility, I can continue to share God's word even in the face of opposition, trusting that the Holy Spirit will work through me to overcome resistance and bring about transformation.

Humble in spirit, meekness enables me to prioritize the well-being of others above my own interests. In Philippians 2:3-4, Paul encourages me to consider others' needs above my own, a mindset that's only possible through meekness. Like Moses, who interceded on behalf of the Israelites despite their rebellion, meekness prompts me to sacrificially serve others and seek their spiritual restoration.

Yet, meekness isn't always easy. In Numbers 20:1-12, Moses' lack of meekness resulted in consequences when he struck the rock in frustration instead of speaking to it as God commanded. Despite this, when the same people later asked him to intercede for them in Numbers 21:4-9, Moses demonstrated humility and obedience, highlighting the importance of meekness in spiritual leadership and restoration.

Meekness also fosters a teachable spirit, allowing me to receive and embrace God's truth with humility and openness.

In Acts 18:24-28, Apollos exemplified meekness by allowing Aquila and Priscilla to teach him, even though he was already knowledgeable in Scripture. This willingness to learn and grow is essential for spiritual maturity and unity within the body of Christ.

Ultimately, meekness isn't just a character trait—it's a way of life that reflects Christ's humility and selflessness. As I cultivate meekness in my heart, I position myself to receive God's blessings and fulfill His purposes for my life. By embracing meekness, I can navigate life's challenges with grace and integrity, trusting in God's strength to sustain me and lead me in paths of righteousness.

Meekness isn't something that just happens—it's a quality I need to actively cultivate in my life. One way I can do this is through fasting, which helps me deny the desires of my flesh and humble myself before God. David, in Psalm 35:13, found strength in fasting, recognizing that food can be a stumbling block that keeps us from God's best for our lives. Just as Adam and Eve, the nation of Israel, Esau, and even Jesus faced temptation related to food, fasting can help me develop self-control and meekness in this area.

Tests and trials also play a crucial role in cultivating meekness. Moses, after spending 40 years in the wilderness, learned humility and dependence on God, despite his previous education and upbringing in the Egyptian court. Jesus, too, learned obedience through suffering, demonstrating the importance of humility and obedience as forms of meekness.

MEEKNESS OR KINDNESS

The Israelites, however, failed to learn from their trials and remained rebellious, highlighting the need for a humble and obedient heart.

Looking to the example of Paul, I see how meekness is demonstrated in the midst of trials. Despite facing numerous hardships, Paul relied on God for comfort and strength rather than turning to his own resources or the help of others. This reliance on God in times of difficulty is a key aspect of cultivating meekness in my own life.

Furthermore, meekness is cultivated through self-denial. A meek person is not focused on themselves but instead prioritizes humility and service to others. Jesus exemplified this self-denial in Philippians 2:5-8, where he emptied himself and took on the form of a servant. This act of humility and submission serves as a model for me as I seek to cultivate meekness in my own heart.

Ultimately, meekness is about surrendering myself to God's will and relying on His strength rather than my own.

It's a continual process of denying self, humbling myself before God, and trusting in His provision and guidance. As I actively cultivate meekness in my life through fasting, trials, and self-denial, I can become more like Christ and experience the blessings that come from a humble and obedient heart.

GOODNESS

As I reflect on the fruit of goodness, I'm reminded that it's not something I can manufacture on my own—it flows from the Spirit of God within me. Understanding God's goodness is foundational to cultivating this fruit in my life. He is inherently good, as seen in passages like Exodus 33:18-19 and Psalm 23:6. His goodness encompasses moral virtue, excellence, and benevolence.

Firstly, goodness reflects God's moral virtue and holiness. We're called to emulate this holiness, not in a self-righteous way, but through the transformative power of Christ in us. Despite our imperfections, Christ makes us holy, enabling us to pursue a life of holiness without adopting a judgmental attitude.

Secondly, goodness is tied to excellence. It's not wrong to enjoy the blessings of life, for they stem from God's creation, which He declared to be good. As beings made in God's image, we're inherently good, called to live lives marked by excellence in all we do.

Lastly, goodness embodies benevolence—a desire to bless others as God longs to bless us. Scriptures like Matthew 7:9 and Romans 8:28 reassure us of God's desire to pour out blessings upon us, encouraging us to expect His goodness in our lives and to extend that same goodness to others.

As I consider examples like Galatians 6:1 and the story of the woman caught in adultery in John 8:3-11, I'm challenged to ask myself some crucial questions. Do I embrace my identity as holy in God's sight? Am I committed to living a life of holiness, excellence, and benevolence? Do I actively seek God's blessing and strive to be a blessing to those around me?

Furthermore, I recognize the close relationship between gentleness and goodness. Gentleness is revealed in our kind attitude towards others, while goodness is demonstrated through our kind actions. They are interconnected, with gentleness paving the way for goodness to flourish. Without gentleness, goodness cannot fully manifest, as seen in Ephesians 4:32 and 1 Thessalonians 2:7-9.

Ultimately, I understand that the enemy seeks to steal the fruit of gentleness, knowing that without it, goodness will fade. Therefore, I'm committed to nurturing both gentleness and goodness in my life, knowing that they reflect the character of Christ and empower me to be a light in the world.

As I ponder the functions of gentleness and goodness in my life, I realize that they play a crucial role in shaping me into the salt of the earth, as Jesus described believers. Just as salt adds flavor and preserves, gentleness and goodness should flavor my interactions with others and preserve the message of God's love in the world. I see now that my behavior should reflect God's kindness and goodness, serving as a tangible expression of His character to those around me.

Moreover, I understand that gentleness and goodness should characterize my actions consistently, regardless of the circumstances or the people I encounter. Just as salt remains the same wherever it is, I should demonstrate kindness to everyone—whether they're believers or not. I'm reminded of the wisdom in James 2:9, urging me not to show favoritism but to treat everyone with the same kindness and respect.

Furthermore, I recognize the cleansing effect that gentleness and goodness can have on my speech. As these fruits develop in my heart, they should manifest in the words I speak. Scriptures like Ephesians 4:29 and Colossians 4:6 challenge me to ensure that my speech is always gracious and edifying. I understand now the importance of speaking words that build up and encourage others, rather than tearing them down. If kindness is lacking in my life, it will inevitably be evident in my speech, highlighting the need to cultivate gentleness and goodness in all aspects of my life.

As I reflect on the purpose of the fruit of goodness, I realize its profound impact on my interactions with others and the world around me. Scriptures like Proverbs 15:1 remind me that kindness has the power to turn away wrath, diffusing tense situations and promoting peace. Additionally, kindness serves as a barrier against gossip, preventing the spread of harmful rumors and protecting relationships from damage, as highlighted in Proverbs 18:8.

I'm struck by the realization that my words possess immense power—they can either wound hearts or bring healing and happiness, as Proverbs 18:20 and 16:24 illustrate. This understanding compels me to choose my words carefully, ensuring that they build others up rather than tear them down. Moreover, goodness acts as a shield against strife, preventing conflicts from escalating and spreading like wildfire, as described in Proverbs 26:20.

As I consider Jesus' teachings in Matthew 5:15-16, I'm reminded of the importance of allowing the light of kindness to shine brightly in my life. Just as a candle illuminates its surroundings, my acts of kindness should radiate God's love and bring glory to Him. However, I realize that there may be "bushels" that threaten to cover this light, hindering the manifestation of gentleness and goodness. Therefore, my focus should be on removing anything that obstructs the expression of kindness in my life, ensuring that my light continues to shine brightly for all to see.

FAITHFULNESS

As I delve into the concept of faithfulness, I can't help but see its close relationship with faith itself. Faith, often depicted as belief in action, is the foundation upon which faithfulness is built. It's not merely about holding a set of beliefs but actively living them out, relying on the guidance and empowerment of the Holy Spirit every step of the way.

In Galatians 5:22, faithfulness is described as encompassing a sense of decency, duty, and trustworthiness, even in the face of severe temptation. This definition resonates deeply with me, as it underscores the importance of steadfastness and reliability in my walk with God. It's about remaining true to my convictions and commitments, even when the world around me pulls me in different directions.

As I reflect on the concept of faithfulness, I'm reminded of the countless examples of faithfulness displayed throughout

FAITHFULNESS

Scripture. From Abraham's unwavering trust in God's promises to Ruth's loyalty to her mother-in-law Naomi, these stories serve as inspiring reminders of the power of faithfulness in the face of adversity.

But faithfulness isn't just about grand gestures or monumental acts of loyalty—it's also about the small, everyday choices I make to honor God and others. It's about showing up consistently, being dependable in my relationships, and faithfully stewarding the resources and gifts that God has entrusted to me.

One aspect of faithfulness that particularly resonates with me is its role in building and maintaining trust. When I consistently demonstrate faithfulness in my words and actions, I foster an environment of trust and reliability in my relationships. Whether it's honoring my commitments, keeping confidences, or standing by those in need, my faithfulness serves as a testament to my character and integrity.

At times, remaining faithful can be challenging, especially when faced with trials, temptations, or uncertainties. Yet, it's during these moments that my faith is truly put to the test. Will I continue to trust God's promises and remain steadfast in my commitment to Him, even when the path ahead seems uncertain? Will I hold fast to my beliefs and values, even in the face of opposition or adversity?

As I navigate the ups and downs of life, I'm constantly reminded of the importance of relying on God's strength and guidance to cultivate and sustain faithfulness in my life. It's through prayer, studying God's Word, and leaning on the support of fellow believers that I find the courage and resilience to remain faithful, even when the journey is challenging.

Faithfulness is not just a character trait—it's a way of life, rooted in a deep and abiding trust in God. It's about living out my beliefs with integrity and reliability, even when faced with difficulties or uncertainties. As I continue to walk in faithfulness, I trust that God will honor my commitment and use me to make a meaningful impact in the world around me.

FAITHFULNESS

GENTLENESS

Gentleness, one of the fruits of the Spirit, is like a rare jewel shining through the character of Christ. While it's mentioned only once in the New Testament, its essence permeates the life of Jesus, illustrating humility and submission to God's will. As I ponder Philippians 2:1-11, I see that gentleness is not just a passive trait but an active choice to live in alignment with God's purpose.

Reflecting on Jesus's life, I'm struck by moments like His baptism and His agonizing prayer in Gethsemane. In both instances, He demonstrated profound gentleness, surrendering to God's plan despite the challenges ahead. It's a reminder that true gentleness stems from a deep trust in God's sovereignty.

Moreover, gentleness extends to how we treat others, whether they're strangers, authorities, fellow believers, or those who haven't embraced Christ. Jesus's interactions with

GENTLENESS

various individuals exemplify this, showing kindness even in the face of criticism and judgment. It challenges me to consider how I respond to people in different circumstances, whether I extend grace or judgment.

Yet, gentleness isn't weakness; it's a powerful force that can disarm hostility and bring healing. Proverbs 25:15 illustrates this beautifully, highlighting the impact of a gentle response in diffusing conflict and calming turbulent situations.

As I delve deeper into understanding gentleness, I'm confronted with introspective questions. Do I genuinely seek God's will for my life, even when it doesn't align with my own desires? How do I handle disagreements and adversity, both with God and with others? Am I known for my gentleness, or do I often react harshly in challenging situations?

The concept of goodness, closely tied to gentleness, underscores the multifaceted nature of this fruit. It encompasses excellence, virtue, kindness, and benevolence, reflecting God's character in its entirety. As I strive to cultivate gentleness in my life, I'm reminded of the transformative power of embodying Christ's likeness in all aspects of my being.

TEMPERANCE OR SELF-CONTROL

Temperance, or self-control, is more than just a concept—it's a practice rooted in power and strength. Derived from the Greek word "enkrateia," it embodies qualities like possessing mastery over desires, exercising discipline, and making wise judgments. In essence, it's about holding the reins of our passions and impulses, steering them in the right direction.

In today's fast-paced world, the need for self-control is ever more pressing. We're bombarded with temptations at every turn, and amidst the hustle and bustle, it's easy to lose sight of the importance of self-mastery. But to be self-controlled means acknowledging the existence of a self that needs taming—the selfish, prideful aspects that lurk within us all. It requires recognizing that human nature, left unchecked, can only be subdued by a force greater than itself.

TEMPERANCE OR SELF-CONTROL

Self-control isn't just about restraining from negative behaviors; it's also about surrendering to a higher authority—the kingdom rule of Jesus Christ. It's about turning away from harmful actions and replacing them with positive ones. For instance, instead of criticizing, we choose to encourage; instead of manipulating, we choose to love wholeheartedly.

The term "exercise" often precedes self-control, and rightly so. Just as physical exercise strengthens our muscles, regularly practicing self-control strengthens our character. Each time we choose self-control over indulgence, we're building discipline and resilience. It's a gradual process of growth—one where each decision to do what's right contributes to the development of our character and ultimately shapes our destiny.

We possess the fruit of self-control within us, but its potency lies in our deliberate choice to exercise it. If we neglect to nurture it, other ungodly attitudes and actions will continue to hold sway over us. But by intentionally making decisions aligned with righteousness, we allow the fruit of self-control to flourish and exert its influence over our lives.

So, let's commit to exercising self-control in every aspect of our lives. With each conscious choice to do what's right, we're reinforcing the strength of this fruit within us, paving the way for greater discipline and spiritual growth.

Temperance empowers me to crucify my flesh, aligning with the call in Galatians 5:24 to live beyond the dictates of my earthly desires. It's not through my own efforts alone that I overcome the flesh; rather, it's the supernatural seed of strength and self-control planted within me.

Drawing inspiration from 1 Corinthians 9:24-27, I liken the journey of mastering self-control to training for the Olympics. Just as athletes meticulously watch their diet and regulate their sleep to achieve peak performance, I must discipline my body and mind to overcome any obstacles hindering me from living my best life in Christ.

Crucial to this discipline is bringing my body under subjection, as highlighted in 1 Corinthians 9:27. Failure to exercise self-control has led many astray, rendering them castaways—rejected and worthless in their spiritual pursuits. Reflecting on 1 Corinthians 10:1-12, I see how Israel's lack of self-control led them astray, succumbing to the lust of the flesh and incurring God's displeasure.

Yet, there's hope amidst temptation, as stated in 1 Corinthians 10:13. While temptation may be inevitable, yielding to it is not. When I lack self-control, I realize that I'm committing spiritual adultery against God, as depicted in Hosea 6:10. It's a sobering reminder of the gravity of self-indulgence and the need to uphold righteousness and godliness, as instructed in Titus 2:11-12.

In essence, temperance is my ally in the battle against worldly desires. It's the key to living a life marked by spiritual discipline, righteousness, and sobriety. Through self-control, I

TEMPERANCE OR SELF-CONTROL

affirm my allegiance to Christ and honor the grace bestowed upon me, striving to live in accordance with His will each day.

Developing temperance requires a concerted effort to control our speech, as highlighted in James 3:2-4 and various proverbs. Words hold immense power, capable of both building up and tearing down. By mastering our tongues, we exercise restraint and cultivate self-control.

Central to strengthening our inner selves is the battle between the flesh and the spirit, as outlined in Galatians 5:16-17. Whichever aspect of ourselves we feed the most will ultimately dominate our lives. Through yielding to the Holy Spirit, we empower ourselves to assert control over the impulses of the flesh. This process mirrors Paul's prayer for the Ephesian believers, emphasizing the importance of inner strength derived from spiritual nourishment.

To fortify our inner selves, we rely on various sources of divine empowerment. Firstly, immersing ourselves in the Word of God equips us with wisdom and discernment, as described in 2 Peter 1:5-6. Additionally, engaging in prayer and worship, including the practice of speaking in tongues, fosters spiritual growth and resilience, as noted in 1 Corinthians 14:4 and Jude 20. Even praise, as exemplified in Psalm 8:2, serves as a conduit for divine strength, aligning us with God's purposes and empowering us to exercise temperance.

Furthermore, temperance is nurtured through the grace of God, as elucidated in Romans 5:1-2. By embracing God's grace, we gain access to His divine strength and enablement. Through prayer, we tap into this wellspring of grace, drawing nearer to God and receiving the self-control needed to fulfill His will. Standing in the grace of God positions us to develop temperance and align our actions with His divine purposes.

Ultimately, as we walk in the Spirit and allow the fruit of the Spirit to blossom in our lives, the constraints of the law lose their power to condemn us. These fruits—love, joy, peace, patience, kindness, goodness, faithfulness, gentleness, and temperance—serve as a moral portrait of Christ Himself. Through our union with Him, His character is reflected in us, empowering us to live lives characterized by self-control and spiritual maturity.

CONCLUSION

As I reflect on our journey through this book "Spiritual Abundance: Unlocking the Power of the Holy Spirit Gifts and Nurturing His Fruit," I am overwhelmed by the depth of revelation and transformation we've experienced together. Throughout our exploration, we've uncovered the profound truth that the Holy Spirit is not only a source of power but also a catalyst for growth and abundance in our spiritual lives.

The nine gifts of the Spirit, as outlined in 1 Corinthians 12:7-11, serve as manifestations of the Spirit's presence and power in our lives. From words of wisdom to the working of miracles, each gift is given for the benefit of all, equipping us to fulfill our unique calling and purpose in the Body of Christ. As the Spirit distributes these gifts according to His will, we are invited to embrace them with humility and gratitude,

CONCLUSION

recognizing their potential to bring about transformation and impact in our lives and communities.

In addition to the gifts of the Spirit, we've also explored the nurturing of His fruit—the nine virtues that reflect the character of Christ Himself. Love, joy, peace, patience, kindness, goodness, faithfulness, gentleness, and self-control are not merely attributes to aspire to but essential components of a life lived in alignment with the Holy Spirit. As we cultivate these fruits in our lives, we become vessels of His love and grace, radiating His light to a world in need.

Our journey through "Spiritual Abundance" has been marked by moments of revelation, empowerment, and deepening intimacy with the Holy Spirit. From the initial understanding of His gifts to the ongoing cultivation of His fruit, each step has brought us closer to the heart of God and His purposes for our lives. As we continue to unlock the power of His gifts and nurture His fruit within us, may we walk in the fullness of His presence and purpose, bringing glory to His name and ushering in His kingdom on earth as it is in heaven.

I am grateful for the opportunity to embark on this journey together, and I am confident that the seeds planted during our time together will continue to bear fruit in the days and years to come. May we remain steadfast in our pursuit of spiritual abundance, trusting in the guidance and empowerment of the Holy Spirit every step of the way. Let us go forth with boldness, knowing that He who began a good work in us will carry it on to completion until the day of Christ Jesus. Amen.

www.ingramcontent.com/pod-product-compliance
Lightning Source LLC
Chambersburg PA
CBHW011613290426
44110CB00020BA/2582